Always grateful for your expert help, Bill!

Too Big?
How To Tell
and
How To Get More Accountability

Bruce D. Thatcher

History Speaks Today
New Braunfels, Texas

BookLocker
Trenton, Georgia

D1590653

Print ISBN: 978-1-958889-67-1
Ebook ISBN: 979-8-88531-497-8

Published by BookLocker.com, Inc., Trenton, Georgia.

Printed on acid-free paper.

BookLocker.com, Inc.
2023

First Edition

Library of Congress Cataloguing in Publication Data
Thatcher, Bruce D.
Too Big? How To Tell and How To Get More Accountability by Bruce D. Thatcher
Library of Congress Control Number: 2023907506

DISCLAIMER

This book details the author's personal experiences with and opinions about accountability of persons in powerful positions. The author is not a licensed legal or psychological professional.

The author and publisher are providing this book and its contents on an "as is" basis and make no representations or warranties of any kind with respect to this book or its contents. The author and publisher disclaim all such representations and warranties including, for example, warranties and advice for a particular purpose. In addition, the author and publisher do not represent or warrant that the information accessible via this book is accurate, complete or current.

Except as specifically stated in this book, neither the author or publisher, nor any authors, contributors, or other representatives will be liable for damages arising out of or in connection with the use of this book. This is a comprehensive limitation of liability that applies to all damages of any kind, including (without limitation) compensatory; direct, indirect or consequential damages; loss of data, income or profit; loss of or damage to property and claims of third parties.

This book provides content related to historical and political topics. As such, use of this book implies your acceptance of this disclaimer.

The History Speaks Today Series

History is recorded and presented by historians, but its lessons must be deduced and applied by political scientists and others. In school, history courses usually focus on a specific country or area, and march through a specific time period in chronological fashion. Who, what, when, where and, maybe, why are covered. So What? is rarely considered.

History's lessons might better be learned by focusing on explicit lessons for the present. Students of business study history in the form of case studies to illustrate what worked and what didn't work, thus creating guides for successful business management. Continuing education in business is almost exclusively 'history' in the form of case study.

History Speaks Today (www.historyspeakstoday.com) applies this approach to historical lessons. Books in the series present overarching lessons, each advanced and then supported by historical episodes and relevant facts. Each book concludes with a summary of the lesson(s) and a discussion of how they might be applied today.

As with business, given similar circumstances and personages, decisions similar to those made in the past will lead to similar outcomes in our time.

History Speaks Today presents explicit guidelines for policymakers in present-day America. Understanding them may not ensure making the best choices today or in the future ... but it will make us better able to reject demonstrated bad choices and, thus, more likely arrive at better choices.

The ten books in the History Speaks Today series are:

Adamant Aggressors: How to Recognize and Deal with Them

What We Learn From Mehmed II of The Ottoman Empire
About Dealing With an *Adamant Aggressor*

What We Learn From James K. Polk of The USA
About Dealing With an *Adamant Aggressor*

What We Learn From Adolph Hitler of Nazi Germany
About Dealing With an Adamant Aggressor

What We Learn From Chaim Weizmann and David Ben-Gurion of Israel *About Dealing With an Adamant Aggressor*

What We Learn From Joseph Stalin of Communist USSR
About Dealing With an Adamant Aggressor

Immigration: How to Avoid its Perils and Make it Work

Rise & Decline: Where We Are and What We Can Do About It

Gun Mania: A New Perspective. What We Must Do to Reduce Shootings, Homicides and Suicides in America

Too Big? How To Tell and How To Get More Accountability

You can buy these books in e-book or print formats from publishers and retailers, or direct from *History Speaks Today*. See direct links at https://www.historyspeakstoday.com/Purchase-HST-Books.php.

Acknowledgments

Many individuals helped me develop, write and publish this work. I'm grateful for all their inputs and suggestions.

Long-time friend Bill Shaffer has again painstakingly copy-edited my manuscript, nudging me toward more interest and consistency in writing style and challenging me along the way.

Special thanks go to those unnamed persons with particular knowledge about specific cases who helped me be sure of the facts about those cases.

My daughter developed and has been administering the History Speaks Today website since its inception -- often investing nighttime hours. Thank you, Shon, for making it work so well, and for keeping it up to date.

Most of all, the support of my beloved wife, Carol, has fueled the entire History Speaks Today project. Without that, neither HST nor this book would ever have progressed beyond the embryonic idea.

To The Reader

Sages from down through the ages tell us that those who fail to learn the lessons of history are doomed to repeat it. But, such lessons are often hard to get at; they're obscured within a great mass of historical detail. *Too Big?* is designed to make it easy for you to get its lessons, regardless of how limited or not your time may be. Try one of these approaches:

Take-Away Synopsis

Read just the Preface, Chapter 21 (Conclusions) and Chapter 22 (What To Do About It) to get a complete articulation of the lessons.

Add Summary Background

To the Preface and Chapters 21 and 22, add the Executive Summaries preceding each case to see how power without significant accountability has corrupted talented leaders of five organizations and led to unnecessary evils.

Detailed Validation

Read the whole book, but skip the Executive Summaries. The historical narrative and Analysis and Discussion for each case add details and documentation to provide a complete picture.

Understanding history's lessons won't guarantee that we'll make the best choices today or in the future. But, understanding these lessons will make us better able to reject demonstrated bad choices and, thus, more likely arrive at better decisions.

Contents

Case 5: Mark Zuckerberg/Facebook-Meta

Conclusions and Current Applications

Sign on the desk of President Harry S Truman (1945-1953)

Preface

Big business, big government, big oil, big tech ... big enough to get the job done ... too big for one's britches, too big to fail, too big to ignore, too big to hide, too big ...

Most groups are formally organized into a hierarchy topped with a recognized leader. Effective functioning requires communication down and up the hierarchy. Communication downward confers under-standing and responsibilities for implementing the purposes of the organization. Communication upward includes accountability – acknowledging directions, reporting and owning subsequent actions.

Countless leadership books discuss accountability in terms of personal, management and business development. Some books address accountability of a corporation or government entity to ethical/moral standards, the public, the law, etc. Less has been written about per-sonal accountability of powerful business, government and other organization leaders in America.

Power is necessary for much human accomplishment, but "power tends to corrupt ... "[a] Accountability works to contain the corruption of power. Its absence enables power to become, almost inevitably, absolute corruption. History has shown that this maxim generally holds for virtually all human activity, including governments, business enterprises, religious and charitable entities, labor unions, political parties and others.

Brilliant and willful individuals marshal resources and people in support of particular ends. They often function as autocrats. They

---

[a] Lord Acton, member of British Parliament, in 1887 letter to Bishop Mandell Creighton.

establish hierarchies below them organized to efficiently implement their ambitions.

As a group grows in resources and strength, the power available to its leader also grows. However egalitarian that person may initially be, power shifts perspective toward the amoral. Power may be specific and effectively limited, or it may be effectively unlimited.

The danger of unchecked power vested in a single person has been recognized for millennia. Different approaches have been used to limit or control it: distributing mechanisms such as a constitution, opposing forces such as nobility vs kings, laws and regulations, elections, etc. Throughout history, the most successful examples of such mechanisms have always included one overriding factor – effective accountability.

Accountability: Obligation to account for one's acts; acceptance of responsibility, and more.

Subordinate: Person who is accountable.

Superior: Person to whom subordinate is accountable.

Effective accountability includes six critical conditions:

1. The responsibilities of the subordinate must be unambiguous, both as to duties and authority, and as to limitations.

2. The superior-subordinate relationship must be personal. One can't be effectively accountable to the public, the Party, the Organization, the Company, the employees, the community, or anything other than an identifiable human person. And groups cannot be truly accountable; only the persons who head them – Presidents, CEOs, Chairmen of the Board, Cabinet Secretaries, etc. and their employees – can be truly accountable.

NOTE 1: A CEO of some sort, at the top of most organizations, is accountable to a board of directors. An elected official is accountable nominally to the voting public.

NOTE 2: Virtually all are theoretically accountable to the law. But that relationship is effective only as regards those who choose to obey law, and only as regards the laws they choose to obey.

3. The superior-subordinate relationship must be one-to-one. Shared accountability is watered down so that no "one" is responsible, and to have more than one boss is to have none; one cannot effectively serve two masters.

4. The superior-subordinate relationship must include timely direct communication between superior and subordinate. Long time lags diminish accountability.

5. The subordinate must not wield control or undue influence over people to whom he or she is accountable.

6. The superior must have real authority to censure, restrain or otherwise affect the subordinate's well-being up to and including employment termination or legal action.

Examples of clear accountability relationships include:

Child – Parent
Student – Teacher
Player – Coach
Employee – Supervisor

Accountability can be traced from low-level employees to the Chief Executive Officer (CEO) within hierarchical organizations such as Amazon, Exxon, the FBI, the Party, Planned Parenthood, the Teamsters, and other organized groups. Because *groups* cannot be truly accountable, the person who heads a group should be accountable for that group's actions. But to whom?

Examples of problematic accountability relationships include:

CEO – Board of Directors
Director(s) – Stockholders
Head of Independent Agency – a segment of the public
Elected Official – Voters
All of the above – Statutory law

The organization typically has vastly more resources available to its leader than those against whose interests she/he may choose to act. History is replete with examples. History is also replete with examples of attempts to control organizations through agreements, laws and regulations.

Organizations may be subjected to financial penalties for wrongdoing, and punishments for violating some laws can be extreme – nationalization, break-up, divestiture. But the individuals acting in the name of the organization often or usually experience no significant penalties for violations of law or regulations on behalf of the organization. And though ignorance of law/rules/underlings' actions should not be a release from accountability, "plausible deniability" is widely put forth as a shield and accepted as an extenuating factor.

Analyses of historical cases reveal many of the ways accountability may be lacking, ineffectively designed, frustrated or avoided. Analysis also reveals where changes might have made accountability more specific and effective. Relevant conclusions include suggestions for new concepts to significantly improve account-ability of organizations in America.

Case Studies

Extensive writings about private and public organizations let us examine how lack of accountability led to amoral use of great power in furthering the interests of the organizations' leaders. From such examinations we can derive applicable principles and suggest what might be done to improve accountability in America.

Cases involving historical figures show these lessons, as do cases involving persons currently in the news. Many current big names in social media and internet commerce including leaders of Facebook, Twitter, Amazon and the like are almost certainly eligible for inclusion. From such an array we have selected five cases to demonstrate enduring principles.

- Robert Clive/East India Company: 1744-1772
- John D. Rockefeller/Standard Oil Company: 1870-1911
- Ralph J. Cordiner/General Electric Company: 1950 -1963
- J. Edgar Hoover/Federal Bureau of Investigation: 1924-1972
- Mark Zuckerberg/Facebook-Meta: 2004-Present

Caution: *Examine each case with absolute dispassion.* Resist the urge to make moral judgments, however justified. Applying moral values will tend to cloud lessons to be learned. Remain objective.

Case 1:

Robert Clive/East India Company

Chapter 1:
Executive Summary

At its formation, EIC founders invested "for the honour of our native country and for the advancement of trade and merchandise within this realm of England." In addition to these strictly commercial purposes, in 1600 the official Charter of the East India Company included "authority to rule territories and raise armies."

Such authority lay dormant for almost a century until, in the 1680s, a new Director of EIC in India decided to militarily force the Mughals to accept his dominance. He arranged for English warships and soldiers to sail to Bengal for that purpose. However, the Mughal war machine swept them away, captured and closed many EIC factories and expelled the East India Company from Bengal. After several years, in 1690, the Mughal emperor allowed EIC to return.

Corruption in the service of Company interests had by then become standard practice. By 1693, in London, the East India Company was routinely buying members of Parliament, ministers, the Solicitor General and the Attorney General. Investigation found "EIC guilty of bribery and insider trading and led to the impeachment of the Lord President of the Council and the Imprisonment of the Company's Governor."

In 1700, the East India Company began to enforce its will arbitrarily in India. By 1701, a Mughal governor was complaining EIC had rendered "no account of their administration … nor had they accounted for the revenues from tobacco, betel, wine et cetera." EIC responded that if the governor was harsh and overtaxed them, they would move EIC operations elsewhere.

Nine years later they took up arms.

... factors of Fort St David ... laid waste to fifty-two towns and villages along the Coromandel coast, killing innocent villagers and destroying crops ... perhaps the first major act of violence by Englishmen against the ordinary people ... The Directors in London approved of the measures taken ...

In Bengal, Murshid Quli Khan had also become disgusted by the rudeness and bullying of ... (EIC) officials in Calcutta and wrote to Delhi ...

"When they first came to this country they petitioned ... in a humble manner for the liberty to purchase a spot of ground to build a factory house upon, which was no sooner granted but they ran up a strong fort ... They rob and plunder and carry a great number of the king's subjects of both sexes into slavery."

In 1743, at the age of 18, Robert Clive was sent to Madras in the service of the East India Company.

The Company was then purely a trading corporation ... rent was paid to the native governments. Its troops were scarcely numerous enough to man the batteries of three or four ill-constructed forts, which had been erected for the protection of the warehouses. The business of the servants of the Company was ... to take stock, to make advances to weavers, to ship cargoes, and above all to keep an eye on private traders ... the younger clerks were so miserably paid that they could scarcely subsist without incurring debt; the elder enriched themselves by trading on their own account; and those who lived to rise to the top of the service often accumulated considerable fortunes.

Clive arrived at Madras in 1744. The next year, during the War of the Austrian Succession, he was trained to fight and became lieutenant of a Company of infantry. When the war ended in 1749, continuing French harassment led EIC Directors in London to give orders "to make yourselves as secure as you can against the French or any other European Enemy."

In 1751 a Mughal French ally besieged his British-connected rival in the fortress of Trichinopoly and effectively isolated Madras. Clive by then had been promoted to Captain and given charge of two hundred English soldiers and three hundred sepoys. They attacked the Mughal camp by surprise, slaughtered many, dispersed the rest and returned to quarters. But Clive knew the victory was temporary. To relieve the siege he attacked Arcot, the capital of the Carnatic. The battle of Arcot continued for months. By November, Clive and his sepoys won. Madras was secure.

Soon after, Clive married and returned to England as a hero. He had accumulated a small fortune while commissary to the British troops.[a] However, he blew most of the money on high living. He even bought a seat in Parliament, but political opposition prevented his keeping it.

In 1755, Clive rejoined the East India Company, which appointed him governor of Fort St. David in India. Also, the King commissioned him lieutenant-colonel in the British Army, and he sailed for Madras.

In 1756 the Mughal nawab of Bengal captured EIC's fort at Calcutta; news of Calcutta's capture reached Madras in August. With 900 English and 1,500 Indian sepoys, Clive sailed with Admiral Charles Watson to Bengal and retook Calcutta on January 2, 1757.

> On 3 January, Clive declared war on Siraj ud-Daula in the name of the Company; Watson did the same in the name of the Crown. It was the first time that the EIC had ever formally declared war on an Indian prince.

By February 5th Clive and Watson had defeated Siraj ud-Daula. The Treaty of Alinigar signed on February 9 restored all the Company's privileges, paid compensation, allowed EIC to re-fortify Calcutta and establish a mint.

---

[a]   Such commissaries functioned as middlemen, buying supplies and reselling them to the military/navy, usually at grossly-inflated prices.

Clive and Watson were eager to return to Madras, but news of the new 'Seven Years War' in Europe had reached Watson. He was ordered to attack French interests, so the two forces remained in Bengal. They attacked a French trading colony north of Calcutta and ousted the French.

Soon after, Clive was asked by Mīr Ja'far, a general in the Nawab of Bengal's regime, for Company aid in a coup against the Nawab. He "offered the Company the vast sum of 2.5 crore" (£812.5 million, today). The planned coup was, in reality, a conspiracy of Bengal bankers and merchants and parts of the Nawab's military. EIC forces would defeat the Nawab and install the general as the new Nawab of Bengal.

> ... the EIC men on the ground were ignoring their strict instructions from London, which were only to repulse French attacks and avoid potentially ruinous wars with their Mughal hosts. But seeing opportunities for personal enrichment as well as political and economic gain for the Company, they dressed up the conspiracy in colours that they knew would appeal to their masters and presented the coup as if it were primarily aimed at excluding the French from Bengal forever.
>
> This is a crucial point. In as far as the EIC, in the shape of its directors, officers and most shareholders, had a corporate will at all, it was for trade yielding maximum profits and a large and steady dividend for themselves and their investors ... the investors consistently abhorred ambitious plans of conquest ... the great schemes of conquest of the EIC in India very rarely originated in Leadenhall Street (EIC's headquarters). Instead, what conquering, looting and plundering took place was almost always initiated by senior Company officials on the spot, who were effectively outside metropolitan control.

It worked. Clive defeated the Nawab on June 23 at the Battle of Plassey. He placed the general on the throne. Clive was appointed British (EIC) Governor of Bengal.

In compensation for losses to EIC and Calcutta citizens, the conspirators paid Clive – "in modern terms, around £232 million, of which £22 million was reserved for Clive." The new Nawab also gave Clive £234,000 in cash, a Mughal title of nobility, and an estate paying annual rental of about £30,000. A flood of corruption thus began.

Clive returned to England in 1760 as a hero. He was made Baron Clive of Plassey in 1762 and was knighted in 1764. He became a member of Parliament, purchased an estate, and tried (unsuccessfully) to carve out a political career.

But Clive was not universally popular at India House, East India Company's London headquarters. One of the EIC directors "remembered with bitterness the audacity with which (Clive) had repeatedly set at nought the authority of the distant Directors of the Company." So, the Directors moved to confiscate the grant of rent from Mīr Jaʿfar, Clive was forced to take them to court. Meanwhile,

> The internal misgovernment of (EIC in India) had reached such a point that it could go no further. What, indeed, was to be expected from a body of public servants exposed to temptation such that ... flesh and blood could not bear it, armed with irresistible power, and responsible only to the corrupt, turbulent, distracted, ill-informed Company, situated at such a distance that the average interval between the sending of a despatch and the receipt of an answer was above a year and a half? Accordingly, during the five years (after) the departure of Clive from Bengal, the misgovernment of the English was carried to a point such as seems hardly compatible with the very existence of society.

East India Company again turned to Clive, appointing him Governor and commander in chief of Bengal. Arriving in Calcutta on

May 3, 1765, he found that the whole Bengal administration was in chaos.

Almost immediately, Clive replaced the Calcutta Council with men he brought from Madras. EIC employees were ordered not to receive significant gifts except by Clive's consent.

Clive installed a puppet Emperor of all Bengal. In return, the Emperor granted East India Company legal authority to collect and spend taxes throughout Bengal and Bihar, sending the Emperor only an annual tribute. Police and magisterial power remained the province of the Nawab of Bengal, who 'assigned' EIC to act for him. Thus the Company became the virtual ruler of India's two richest provinces.

Clive returned to England in 1767. In 1772, Parliament passed the *East India Company Act 1772* to overhaul EIC management. Provisions included:

- Annual dividends, which had often exceeded 100 percent, were limited to 6 percent until all debts were paid.
- Company agents in India were prohibited from engaging in any private trade or accepting presents or bribes from the "natives".
- Warrren Hastings was appointed Governor General of Bengal, Bombay and Madras.

Investigations uncovered corruption within EIC, and Clive was named as instigator of the corruption. He defended himself in Parliament and, in 1773, "Parliament declared that he did render great and meritorious services to his country." A year later, in 1774, Robert Clive died by his own hand, probably suicide.

It can be argued that the East India Company tacitly approved of Robert Clive's actions, from which they profited greatly. But it was the lack of effective accountability that enabled Clive to enrich himself without regard to Company directives or to the hurt and harm done to

Indian people. Most of the five critical accountability conditions were absent in Robert Clive's relationship with the East India Company.

Many of these flaws might have been eliminated had the Company established a single person at headquarters to have executive responsibility for EIC's Indian operations, to whom Robert Clive would then have reported. But the communications time delay would have remained.

Chapter 2:
Anarchy and Corruption

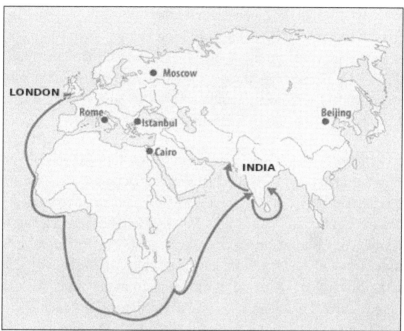

Figure 2-1. The East India Company's trade and communication route between London and India. Sailing times ranged from eight months to a year in each direction.

The East India Company began September 24, 1599, in London as one of the world's first joint stock companies. On that day 101 investors pledged around £30,000 "for the honour of our native country and for the advancement of trade and merchandise within this realm of England."[a] A petition for charter was immediately sent to Queen Elizabeth's Privy Council. On December 31, 1600, the 'Governor and

---

[a] *The Anarchy; The East India Company, Corporate Violence, and the Pillage of an Empire*, Chapter 1, William Dalrymple.

Company of Merchants of London trading to the East Indies' received a Royal Charter. Among its grants to the East India Company were freedom from customs for the first six voyages, a 15-year monopoly over British trade to the East Indies, and authority to rule territories and raise armies.

The East India Company would become, at its peak in the nineteenth century and with operations on every known continent, the most powerful corporation in history. It controlled almost half the world's trade. By 1857 its three presidency armies in India numbered 271,000 officers and mostly Indian soldiers (sepoys), which was more than twice as large as the United Kingdom armed forces.

EIC's principal competitors were chartered by four European powers: Portugal, Holland (Dutch United Provinces). Denmark and France.

Portugal's Vasco da Gama reached the Indian subcontinent and landed at Calicut in May 1498. Portugal established regular trade routes between Europe, India and the far east. The **Portuguese State of India** was founded six years later. Its capital at present-day Cochin was the governing center of Portuguese fortresses and settlements scattered along the Indian coasts and throughout the Indian Ocean. Portugal never developed significant trade with the interior of India. The last Portuguese territory in India was transferred to the Indian government in 1974.

In 1605 the **Dutch East India Company** established a trading outpost at Pulicat. The company ultimately traded textiles, gemstones, indigo, silk, saltpeter, opium and pepper from the Indian subcontinent. It also traded in Indian slaves, which it sold in the Spice Islands and in the Dutch Cape Colony. In the second half of the eighteenth century the Dutch lost much of their influence and, by 1825, their last trading posts in India.

In March 1616, the King of Denmark-Norway issued a charter creating a **Danish East India Company**. Its first expedition reached

India in May 1620, and a treaty signed in November granted rights to build a fort and levy taxes. Early trade was not profitable, so the company was dissolved. A new Danish East India Company formed in 1670, and several commercial outposts were established. In 1729, the King forced the Company to loan him money, which he didn't repay. That and inconsistent Indian trade forced the Company into bankruptcy. Trade continued, but by 1869 Danish presence and trade in India ended.

The **French East India Company** established its first French factory (trading center) in India at Surat in 1668. Until 1741, the Company's objectives were purely commercial. That year French India got a new governor who wanted to establish a territorial empire in India. His hopes ended in 1754 after a defeat by British East India Company forces. Fighting between EIC and the French continued until, in 1769, the by then unprofitable French East India Company was abolished by the French Crown, which assumed administration of French possessions in India.

Fighting between EIC and the French continued intermittently until the end of the Napoleonic wars in 1816. After Indian independence in 1947 French territories in India were gradually transferred to India; the last came under effective India rule in 1954.

Four ships sailed out of London for India in February 1601 to begin the first voyage of the British **East India Company**. In mid-1602 the fleet landed at Acheh and negotiated a deal with the Sultan. Returning to London the fleet attacked a Portuguese ship and added its load of spices to those obtained from the Sultan. It arrived home in mid-1603 with 900 tons of pepper, cinnamon and cloves plus the spices bought in Acheh.[a]

---

[a] Ibid.

EIC struggled to trade in the East Indies against the formidable Dutch. So it shifted its focus to fine cotton textiles, indigo and chintzes from India. The Company landed at Surat in 1608 and began to establish a relationship with the ruling Mughal Emperor. It took years, but in 1615 the Mughal authorized the building of a trading center (factory) at Surat. Thus began a centuries-long partnership between EIC and Mughal emperors for jewels, pepper, textiles and saltpeter. EIC began using and transporting slaves a few years later.

> Beginning in the early 1620s, the East India Company began using slave labour ... Although some of those enslaved by the company came from Indonesia and West Africa, the majority came from East Africa ... and were primarily transported to the company's holdings in India and Indonesia. Large-scale transportation of slaves by the company was prevalent from the 1730s to the early 1750s and ended in the 1770s.[a]

After two unsuccessful ventures, EIC negotiated successfully in 1632 to build a settlement with a fort and 'castle' at Madras, with no customs duties to be charged for 30 years.

> Soon weavers and other artificers and traders began pouring in. Still more came once the fort walls had been erected ... the people up and down the coast were looking for exactly the security and protection the Company could provide.
> Before long Madras had grown to become the first English colonial town in India with its own small civil administration ... and a population of 40,000. By the 1670s the town was even minting its own gold 'pagoda' coins.[b]

The second English settlement in India was the island of Bumbye (Bombay), which England captured from Portugal and turned over to

---

[a] Encyclopædia Britannica, East India Company.
[b] *The Anarchy; The East India Company, Corporate Violence, and the Pillage of an Empire*, Chapter 1, William Dalrymple.

the East India Company. Settlement (finally) began in 1665. Within 30 years Bombay had a colonial population of 60,000.

In the 1680s a new Director was appointed head of EIC in India. He decided to militarily force the Mughals to accept his dominance. Bad decision. In 1686, English warships with cannons and soldiers sailed to Bengal. The Mughal war machine swept them away. Soon EIC factories at many locations had been captured, EIC had been expelled from Bengal, the Surat factory was closed and Bombay was blockaded.

In 1690 the Mughal emperor finally let the Company come back. That same year EIC bought the future site of Calcutta.

By 1693, back in London, East India Company was regularly bribing parliamentarians, ministers, the Solicitor General and the Attorney General. Investigation found "the EIC guilty of bribery and insider trading and led to the impeachment of the Lord President of the Council and the Imprisonment of the Company's Governor."[a] It was a harbinger of things to come.

In 1700, India, under Mughal Emperor Aurangzeb, account(ed) for 27 per cent of the world economy.[b] However, because of warring among Indian rulers, Mughals no longer could exercise firm control. The East India Company began to enforce its will arbitrarily. In 1701, a Mughal governor complained that the Madras Council had rendered "no account of their administration ... nor had they accounted for the revenues from tobacco, betel, wine et cetera."[c] EIC's response was that if the governor was harsh and overtaxed them, they would move the EIC operations elsewhere. Nine years later they took up arms.

> In response to ... a short siege by the Mughar (fort keeper) of Jinji, the factors of Fort St David, a little to the south of

---

[a] Ibid.

[b] *Inglorious Empire; What the British Did to India,* Timeline, Shashi Tharoor.

[c] *The Anarchy; The East India Company, Corporate Violence, and the Pillage of an Empire,* Chapter 1, William Dalrymple.

Madras ... rode out of their fortifications ... broke through
Mughal lines and laid waste to fifty-two towns and villages
along the Coromandel coast, killing innocent villagers and
destroying crops containing thousands of pagodas of rice
awaiting harvest ... perhaps the first major act of violence by
Englishmen against the ordinary people ... The Directors in
London approved of the measures ...

In Bengal, Murshid Quli Khan had also become
disgusted by the rudeness and bullying of ... (EIC) officials
in Calcutta and wrote to Delhi ...

"When they first came to this country they petitioned ...
in a humble manner for the liberty to purchase a spot of
ground to build a factory house upon, which was no sooner
granted but they ran up a strong fort ... and mounted a great
number of guns upon the walls. They have enticed several
merchants and others to go and take protection under them
and they collect a revenue which amounts to (over £1
million today) ... They rob and plunder and carry a great
number of the king's subjects of both sexes into slavery."[a]

But the Mughal Empire was occupied with more serious concerns
– civil wars and invading Persians. By 1737-1739 the empire was
fragmenting and its treasury had been carried off by Persians.

The coastal area from north of Madras southward was a
dependency within the Mughal Empire generally known as the
Carnatic. A series of three wars were fought among regional rulers for
succession and territory between 1742 and 1763. The French intervened in 1742 and, over the next seven years, increased their effective
hold on the area. Their success would be checked in 1751 by EIC
forces led by Robert Clive, the first British administrator of Bengal.
During the Seven Years' War of 1756-1763, both France and England
sent forces to India; the British and their Indian allies won. EIC took

---

[a]   Ibid.

control of the Carnatic through its nawab,[b] who became indebted to the East India Company and to its individual officers.

Robert Clive was born September 29, 1725, in Shropshire, England. In 1743, at the age of 18, he was sent to Madras in the service of the East India Company.

> Some lineaments of the character of the man were early discerned in the child … "Fighting," says one of his uncles, "to which he is out of measure addicted, gives his temper such a fierceness and imperiousness, that he flies out on every trifling occasion" … he formed all the idle lads of the town into a kind of predatory army, and compelled the shopkeepers to submit to a tribute of apples and half-pence, in consideration of which he guaranteed the security of their windows. He was sent from school to school … gaining for himself everywhere the character of an exceedingly naughty boy … the general opinion seems to have been that poor Robert was a dunce, if not a reprobate. His family expected nothing good from … such a headstrong temper. It is not strange therefore, that they gladly accepted for him, when he was in his eighteenth year, a writership in the service of the East India Company, and shipped him off to make a fortune or to die of a fever at Madras.
>
> The Company was then purely a trading corporation. Its territory consisted of a few square miles, for which rent was paid to the native governments. Its troops were scarcely numerous enough to man the batteries of three or four ill-constructed forts, which had been erected for the protection of the warehouses. The natives … were armed, some with swords and shields, some with bows and arrows. The business of the servants of the Company was … to take stock, to make advances to weavers, to ship cargoes, and above all to keep an eye on private traders who dared to infringe the monopoly. The younger clerks were so miserably paid that they could scarcely subsist without

[b] Deputy ruler, or viceroy, under the Mughal rule of India. The title was later adopted by independent rulers of Bengal, Oudh and Arcot.

incurring debt; the elder enriched themselves by trading on their own account; and those who lived to rise to the top of the service often accumulated considerable fortunes.[a]

Robert Clive arrived at Madras in 1744, and spent the next two years as a glorified assistant shopkeeper, tallying books, quarreling with fellow employees, and arguing with suppliers of the East India Company.

> He was lonely, homesick and miserable ... (and) developed a profound hatred for India that never left him ... Within a year ... he turned his innate violence on himself and attempted suicide.
> What he did have ... was a streetfighter's eye for sizing up an opponent, a talent at seizing the opportunities presented by happenchance, a willingness to take great risks and a breathtaking audacity. He was also blessed with a reckless bravery; and, when he chose to exercise it, a dark personal magnetism that gave him power over men.[b]

In September 1745, during the War of the Austrian Succession, French forces besieged and captured Madras. Clive escaped and made his way to Fort St. David, where he was trained to fight and became lieutenant of a Company of foot (infantry).

When the war ended in 1749, Madras was restored to the English. Nevertheless, continuing French harassment led EIC Directors in London to declare to its operatives in India,

> Experience has proved that no regard is paid by the French to the neutrality of the Mogul's Dominions, and ... You have orders to make yourselves as secure as you can against the French or any other European Enemy ... His Majesty will support the Company in whatever they may think fit to do

---

[a]   *Macaulay's Essay On Robert Clive*, III, Thomas Babington Macaulay.
[b]   *The Anarchy; The East India Company, Corporate Violence, and the Pillage of an Empire*, Chapter 2, William Dalrymple.

for their future Security; for though a Peace is now made with France, no one knows how long it may last[a]

The French fomented and intervened in civil wars among Mughals. They achieved effective control of the Carnatic coast. In 1751 Mughal viceroy (governor) Chanda Sahib, an ally of the French, besieged his British-connected rival, Muḥammad Ali, in the fortress of Trichinopoly. Madras was effectively isolated by 1751.

> Clive was now twenty-five years old. After hesitating for some time between a military and a commercial life, he had at length been placed in a post which partook of both characters, that of commissary to the troops, with the rank of captain … He represented to his superiors that unless some vigorous effort were made, Trichinopoly would fall … and the French would become the real masters of the whole peninsula of India. It was absolutely necessary to strike some daring blow. If an attack were made on Arcot, the capital of the Carnatic, and the favourite residence of the Nabobs, it was not impossible that the siege of Trichinopoly would be raised … The young captain was put at the head of two hundred English soldiers, and three hundred sepoys … Clive pushed on … to the gates of Arcot. The garrison, in a panic, evacuated the fort, and the English entered it without a blow.
>
> But Clive well knew that he should not be suffered to retain undisturbed possession of his conquest. He instantly began to … make preparations for sustaining a siege. The garrison … having been swelled by large reinforcements from the neighbourhood to a force of three thousand men, encamped close to the town. At dead of night, Clive marched out of the fort, attacked the camp by surprise, slew great numbers, dispersed the rest, and returned to his quarters without having lost a single man.[b]

---

[a] Ibid, Chapter 1.
[b] *Macaulay's Essay On Robert Clive*, XV, Thomas Babington Macaulay.

The battle of Arcot continued for months. French forces and their Mughal allies besieged Clive and his forces. Clive attacked and besieged the French-Mughal forces. By November 1751 the English and their sepoys won. Madras was secure.

Soon after, being in very poor health, Clive married and returned to England as a hero. He had accumulated a small fortune while commissary to the British troops, some of which he spent on his family. However, he blew most of the money on high living. He even bought a seat in Parliament, but political opposition prevented his keeping it.[a]

The French and Indian Wars in America had begun in late 1752. By 1755, many in Europe presumed that a broader war between England and France was imminent.

> many signs indicated that a war between France and Great Britain was at hand; and it was therefore thought desirable to send an able commander to the Company's settlements in India. The (EIC) Directors appointed Clive governor of Fort St. David. The King gave him the commission of a lieutenant-colonel in the British Army, and in 1755 he again sailed for Asia.[b]

In 1756 the Mughal nawab of Bengal captured the EIC fort at Calcutta. The nawab then allowed the 146 English prisoners to be confined overnight in the prison of the fort, a 20-foot square cell known as "the Black Hole" (of Calcutta). Only 23 prisoners survived the night.

News of Calcutta's capture reached Madras in August. With 900 English and 1,500 Indian sepoys, Clive sailed with Admiral Charles Watson to Bengal and retook Calcutta on January 2, 1757.

---

[a] Ibid, XX- XXI.
[b] Ibid, XXII.

On 3 January, Clive declared war on Siraj ud-Daula in the name of the Company; Watson did the same in the name of the Crown. It was the first time that the EIC had ever formally declared war on an Indian prince[a]

By February 5th the combined forces of Clive and Watson had defeated Siraj ud-Daula. The Treaty of Alinigar signed on February 9th restored all the Company's privileges, paid compensation, allowed EIC to re-fortify Calcutta and establish a mint.

Clive and Watson were eager to return to Madras, but news of the new 'Seven Years War' in Europe had reached Watson. He was ordered to attack French interests, so the two forces remained in Bengal. They attacked Chandernagar a French trading colony north of Calcutta and ousted the French.

Soon after, Mīr Jaʿfar, a general in the Nawab of Bengal's regime, asked Clive for EIC aid in a coup against the Nawab. He "offered the Company the vast sum of 2.5 crore" (£812.5 million, today). The planned coup was, in reality, a conspiracy of Bengal bankers and merchants and parts of the Nawab's military. In return for the general's cooperation, EIC forces would defeat the Nawab and install the general as the new Nawab and (nominal) ruler of Bengal.

This was not part of any imperial master plan. In fact, the EIC men on the ground were ignoring their strict instructions from London, which were only to repulse French attacks and avoid potentially ruinous wars with their Mughal hosts. But seeing opportunities for personal enrichment as well as political and economic gain for the Company, they dressed up the conspiracy in colours that they knew would appeal to their masters and presented the coup as if it were primarily aimed at excluding the French from Bengal forever.

This is a crucial point. In as far as the EIC, in the shape of its directors, officers and most shareholders, had a

---

[a] *The Anarchy; The East India Company, Corporate Violence, and the Pillage of an Empire*, Chapter 3, William Dalrymple.

corporate will at all, it was for trade yielding maximum profits and a large and steady dividend for themselves and their investors ... the investors consistently abhorred ambitious plans of conquest ... the great schemes of conquest of the EIC in India very rarely originated in Leadenhall Street (EIC's headquarters). Instead, what conquering, looting and plundering took place was almost always initiated by senior Company officials on the spot, who were effectively outside metropolitan control.[a]

One of the conspirators, a wealthy Bengalese named Omichund, communicated with the Nawab to allay any apprehensions he might have.

This Omichund had been one of the wealthiest native merchants resident at Calcutta, and had sustained great losses in consequence of the Nabob's expedition against that place ... He possessed great influence with his own race, and had in large measure the Hindoo talents, quick observation, tact, dexterity, perseverance, and the Hindoo vices, servility, greediness, and treachery.[b]

It was impossible that a plot which had so many ramifications should long remain entirely concealed. Enough reached the ears of the Nabob to arouse his suspicions. But he was soon quieted by the fictions and artifices which ... Omichund produced ... All was going well; the plot was nearly ripe; (t)hen Clive learned that Omichund was likely to play false ... He held the thread of the whole intrigue ... The lives of Watts, of Meer Jaffier, of all the conspirators, were at his mercy; and he determined to take advantage of his situation and to make his own terms. He demanded three hundred thousand pounds sterling as the price of his secrecy and of his assistance ... But Clive was more than Omichund's match in Omichund's own arts. The man, he said, was a villain ... The best course would be to promise

---

[a] Ibid.
[b] *Macaulay's Essay On Robert Clive*, XXVII, Thomas Babington Macaulay.

what was asked ... and then they might ... withhold from him, not only the bribe which he now demanded, but also the compensation which all the other sufferers of Calcutta were to receive.

His advice was taken. But how was the wary and sagacious Hindoo to be deceived? He had demanded that an article touching his claims should be inserted in the treaty between Meer Jaffier and the English, and he would not be satisfied unless he saw it with his own eyes. Clive had an expedient ready. Two treaties were drawn up, one on white paper, the other on red, the former real, the latter fictitious. In the former Omichund's name was not mentioned; the latter, which was to be shown to him, contained a stipulation in his favour.

But another difficulty arose. Admiral Watson had scruples about signing the red treaty. Omichund's vigilance and acuteness were such that the absence of so important a name would probably awaken his suspicions. But Clive was not a man to do anything by halves ... He forged Admiral Watson's name.[a]

It worked. With Mīr Ja'far's disengagement, Clive defeated the Nawab on June 23 at the Battle of Plassey, and placed the general on the throne of Bengal. Clive was appointed British (EIC) Governor of Bengal. On July 7 he received payment from the conspirators – "in modern terms, around £232 million, of which £22 million was reserved for Clive."[b]

Clive's first government lasted until February 1760. By 1760 Mīr Ja'far's authority was unchallenged by Indians in Bengal, Bahar, and Orissa, and his subservience to EIC was complete. In addition, by the dispatch of a force under Col. Francis Forde in 1758, Clive secured the Northern Sarkars from the French garrison there.

---

[a] *Macaulay's Essay On Robert Clive*, XXIX, Thomas Babington Macaulay.
[b] Ibid.

From the new Nawab, Clive got compensation for losses to EIC and the Calcutta citizens. The Nawab also gave Clive £234,000[c] in cash, a Mughal title of nobility, and an estate paying annual rental of about £30,000. A flood of corruption thus began. Moreover, the East India Company was exempted from duties on both the company's goods and on the private trade of EIC employees.

Clive returned to England in 1760. He was made Baron Clive of Plassey in 1762 and was knighted in 1764. He became member of Parliament, purchased an estate, and tried (unsuccessfully) to carve out a political career.

But Clive was not universally popular among the directors at the London headquarters of EIC (India House).

> At the head of the preponderating party in the India House, had long stood a powerful, able, and ambitious director of the name of Sulivan. He had conceived a strong jealousy of Clive, and remembered with bitterness the audacity with which the late governor of Bengal had repeatedly set at nought the authority of the distant Directors of the Company ... The whole body of Directors was then chosen annually. At the election of 1763 ... Sulivan was victorious, and hastened to take his revenge. The grant of rent which Clive had received from Meer Jaffier was, in the opinion of the best English lawyers, valid ... The Directors, however, most unjustly determined to confiscate it, and Clive was forced to file a bill in Chancery (take them to court).[b]

> But ... Every ship from Bengal had for some time brought alarming tidings. The internal misgovernment of the province had reached such a point that it could go no further. What, indeed, was to be expected from a body of public servants exposed to temptation such that, as Clive once said, flesh and blood could not bear it, armed with irresistible power, and responsible only to the corrupt, turbulent,

---

[c] £7.6 million today.
[b] *Macaulay's Essay On Robert Clive*, XL, Thomas Babington Macaulay.

distracted, ill-informed Company, situated at such a distance that the average interval between the sending of a despatch and the receipt of an answer was above a year and a half? Accordingly, during the five years which followed the departure of Clive from Bengal, the misgovernment of the English was carried to a point such as seems hardly compatible with the very existence of society.[a]

By 1764 the EIC Calcutta Council was ignoring orders of EIC Governor Henry Vansittart, and the Mughal emperor in India had attacked again. East India Company turned to Clive, appointing him Governor and commander in chief of Bengal with power to override the Calcutta Council. Arriving in Calcutta on May 3, 1765, he found that battles had already been won, and the emperor had joined the British camp. But the whole Bengal administration was in chaos.

Almost immediately, Clive ousted the Calcutta Council and replaced it with men he brought from Madras. EIC employees were ordered not to receive significant gifts except by Clive's consent. Private trade was forbidden, but continued at a reduced level.

Clive installed a puppet Emperor of all Bengal. In return, the Emperor granted East India Company legal authority to collect and spend taxes throughout Bengal and Bihar, sending the Emperor only an annual tribute. Police and magisterial power remained the province of the Nawab of Bengal, who 'assigned' EIC to act for him. Thus the Company became the virtual ruler of India's two richest provinces.

Clive returned to England in 1767. Subsequently, EIC profits plunged, and it failed to meet financial commitments to the Bank of England and the government. In 1772, EIC appealed to Parliament to bail it out, which it did, and also passed the *East India Company Act 1772 (Regulating Act of 1773)* to overhaul EIC management. Provisions included:

---

[a]   Ibid, XLI..

- Annual dividends, which often exceeded 100 percent, were limited to 6 percent until all debts were paid.
- Company agents in India were prohibited from engaging in any private trade or accepting presents or bribes from the "natives".
- Warrren Hastings was appointed Governor General of Bengal, Bombay and Madras.

Investigations uncovered corruption within EIC, and Clive was named as instigator of the corruption. He defended himself in Parliament and, in 1773, "Parliament declared that he did render great and meritorious services to his country."[a] A year later, in 1774, Robert Clive died by his own hand, probably suicide.

Epilogue

The *Regulating Act of 1773* proved generally ineffective. Parliament replaced it with *The East India Company Act 1784,* which was intended to bring EIC's rule in India under control of Parliament. It provided for governing of British India jointly by EIC and the Crown with the government having final authority over acts and operations relating to the civil, military and revenues of the Company.

The Act also stated that "to pursue schemes of conquest and extension of dominion in India are measures repugnant to the wish, the honour and the policy of this nation."

Warren Hastings had been made *de facto* Governor General of Bengal in 1772. He generally continued the actions of Robert Clive. From 1779–1784 he led forces of the East India Company against a strong coalition of native states and the French, and prevailed. France lost its influence in India. (In 1787, Hastings was accused of corruption and impeached, but he was acquitted in 1795.)

---

[a]   Encyclopædia Britannica, East India Company.

In 1786 Lord Cornwallis replaced Hasting as Governor General of Bengal, becoming the effective ruler of British India. A constitution established by *The East India Company Act 1784* would last until 1858, when EIC's rule over India would end.

The first of three Anglo-Maratha wars with the Maratha Empire in the north of India began in 1775. By the time the last ended in 1818 any substantial native power in India had been subdued by British-led forces.

Around 1847, EIC Directors in India promulgated the *Doctrine of Lapse* - an annexation policy applied until 1859. The doctrine provided that any Indian princely state under the suzerainty of the East India Company would be annexed into British India if the ruler was either "manifestly incompetent or died without a male heir".[a] Many small states were brought under EIC rule using this doctrine.

In 1857, EIC sepoys in north and central India rebelled over the use of Enfield cartridges.[b] The rebels were soon joined by Indian nobility, many of whom had lost titles and domains under the *Doctrine of Lapse*. Rebels captured much of the North-Western Provinces and Awadh before EIC and allied Princely states mobilized and suppressed the rebellion in 1858. Shortly thereafter, Parliament nationalized the East India Company.

The *East India Act 1858* called for liquidation of the East India Company and the transference of all its property and other assets to the Crown. The Crown also assumed the responsibilities of the Company as they related to treaties, contracts, and business arrangements.

The Act ushered in the new British Raj. It would last until 1947 when India and Pakistan became independent nations.

---

[a]   *India: A History. Revised and Updated*, Chapter 17. John Keay.
[b]   Enfield cartridges contained tallow, which conflicted with Hindu spiritual beliefs.

Chapter 3:
Analysis and Discussion – Robert Clive/East India Company

The East India Company activities were already rife with corruption when Robert Clive first set foot in India. During his first stint in India Clive had ample opportunity to observe EIC agents engaging in private trades and taking 'gifts' from Indians. He obtained the post of Commissary To The Troops, which included a tolerated corruption through inflated charges to the Army and the Navy. After only seven years in India, Clive returned to England in 1751-52 as a wealthy man.

By 1755, Clive had run through his small fortune and rejoined the East India Company. EIC appointed him governor of Fort St. David in India, and the King commissioned him lieutenant-colonel in the British Army. He was surely aware of EIC's "strict instructions … only to repulse French attacks and avoid potentially ruinous wars with their Mughal hosts." Nevertheless, Clive joined an Indian conspiracy to depose the Nawab of Bengal. The coup was successful. The conspirators paid Clive – "in modern terms, around £232 million, of which £22 million was reserved for Clive." The new Nawab also gave Clive £234,000 in cash, a Mughal title of nobility, and an estate paying annual rental of about £30,000.

When Clive returned to England in 1760 he was an incredibly wealthy man. But after one of the EIC directors "remembered with bitterness the audacity with which (he) had repeatedly set at nought the authority of the distant Directors of the Company," the Directors moved to confiscate his grant of rent from the Mughal. Clive took them to court.

By 1764 operations in India were in such bad shape that the East India Company again turned to Clive, appointing him Governor and commander in chief of Bengal. Arriving in Calcutta in 1765, he installed a puppet Emperor of all Bengal. In return, the Emperor granted East India Company legal authority to collect and spend taxes throughout Bengal and Bihar, sending the Emperor only an annual tribute. EIC was ruthless in collecting taxes, most of which were retained by Company and its agents.

Clive returned to England in 1767. By 1772, Parliament's investigators had uncovered corruption within EIC, and Clive was named as instigator. He defended himself in Parliament and, in 1773, that body "declared that he did render great and meritorious services to his country."

It can be argued that the East India Company tacitly approved of Robert Clive's actions, from which they profited greatly. Even the Directors' actions in 1760 were limited to confiscating some of the payments Clive was receiving from an Indian Mughal. Even the law – Parliament – exonerated Clive of all charges.

But it was the lack of effective accountability that enabled Clive to enrich himself without regard to Company directives or the hurt and harm done to Indian people. Consider that most of the six critical accountability conditions were absent in Robert Clive's relationship with the East India Company.

1. The scope of Clive's responsibilities were not clearly spelled out.

2. There appears to have been no personal superior-subordinate relationship. Nowhere is it found that Clive, in India, ever reported to a specific individual at EIC's London headquarters.

3. There was not a one-to-one superior-subordinate relationship. Clive was theoretically responsible to a group of people – "the Directors" of the East India Company.

4. The long time delay in communications between Clive and headquarters was a huge part of the problem. It took up to a year for communication to travel to or from headquarters.

6. No one individual had authority to censure, restrain or otherwise affect Clive's well-being. Anything Company Directors or Parliament might want to do required a majority vote.

Conclusions

Many of these flaws in accountability might have been eliminated had the East India Company established a single person at headquarters to have executive responsibility for EIC's Indian operations, to whom Robert Clive would then have reported. But the communications time delay would have remained.

Questions to Consider

- Suppose the East India Company had assigned responsibility for Indian operations to a specific person at the London headquarters. How might that have worked? Historically, what might have changed?
- Suppose headquarters officials routinely visited India. Would that have improved accountability?
- Suppose EIC had routinely rotated field Directors of Indian operations on a regular basis. How might this have affected accountability?

- EIC's "younger clerks were so miserably paid that they could scarcely subsist without incurring debt; the elder enriched themselves by trading on their own account; and those who lived to rise to the top of the service often accumulated considerable fortunes." What changes to the compensation system might have improved accountability of the field Directors of Indian operations? Why?

Chapter 4:
Additional Reading – Robert Clive/
East India Company

Dalrymple, William. *The Anarchy: The East India Company, Corporate Violence, and the Pillage of an Empire*. Bloomsbury Publishing, 2019.

Dalrymple, William. *The East India Company: The original corporate raiders. The Guardian*, March 4, 2015.

James, Lawrence. *RAJ: The Making and Unmaking of British India*. Time Warner Books UK, 1997.

Keay, John. *India: A History*. Revised and Updated. Grove Press, 2011

Macaulay, Thomas Babington. Ed. by Richard Wilson. *Macaulay's essay on Robert Clive*. M Dent & Sons, 1920. https://archive.org/ details/macaulaysessayon0000maca/page/n5/mode/2up

Spear, T. Percival. *Encyclopedia Britannica*, Robert Clive. https://www.britannica.com/biography/Robert-Clive.

Tharoor, Shashi. *Inglorious Empire: what the British did to India*. Scribe US, 2018.

Also, search the internet for topics such as: Robert Clive, East India Company, British East India Company, history of India, etc.

Case 2:

John D. Rockefeller/Standard Oil Company

Chapter 5:
Executive Summary

John Davison Rockefeller was born July 8, 1839, on a rude homestead near Richford in upstate New York. By 1854 his family had relocated to Cleveland, Ohio, where he completed a three-month course at a business college. There he learned bookkeeping, which he soon viewed as crucial for success in business, and fundamental principles of business transactions.

Upon graduation, at the age of 16, Rockefeller went to work for Hewitt and Tuttle, commission merchants and produce shippers. He didn't stay long. On April 1, 1858 John and Maurice B. Clark became partners in Clark and Rockefeller, a new commission house that traded in commodities shipping through the port of Cleveland. They were successful, but a discovery less than 100 miles east would soon change the partners' lives and lead to Rockefeller becoming, by the time of his death, the wealthiest American in history.

On August 27, 1859, Edwin Drake struck oil near Titusville, Pennsylvania. An oil rush ensued. Rockefeller didn't join the oil rush. But within a few years he entered the oil business, downstream as a refiner. He was drawn into the business through Maurice Clark's friendship with Samuel Andrews; Andrews, Clark and Co. erected its new refinery just a mile and a half east of downtown Cleveland.

Rockefeller spent many hours at the refinery, but he and the Clark brothers didn't get along so, in 1865, Rockefeller bought out their interest and partnered with Sam Andrews. Their refinery was, by then, the largest in Cleveland.

Henry M. Flagler joined the partnership in 1867. The next year he brokered a secret deal with railroads that rebated 71% of published freight rates in return for a promise to load, ship and unload at least 60 carloads of oil per day. Railroads had long been allowing such volume-discount rebates on shipments of other commodities, but Rockefeller, Andrews and Flagler was the only oil refiner then able to guarantee such volumes. Freight rebates helped the Partnership to reduce its kerosene price from 58 cents/gallon in 1865 to 26 cents/gallon by 1870.

Rockefeller decided that industry conditions called for consolidation and cooperation to limit supply and sustain prices. In January 1870, 'Rockefeller, Andrews and Flagler' was superseded by the Standard Oil Company, with John D. Rockefeller as President.

Rockefeller had tried to get producers to curtail output, but this never worked. There were too many producers and more wells coming on line almost every day. Rockefeller estimated, in 1870, that 90 per cent of all refineries were losing money.

Rockefeller saw that he could control supply and pricing of both crude and refined products if he could consolidate refining capacity. Attendant scale economies in refined products would enable lower prices for consumer sales, and for squeezing competitors targeted for agreement, acquisition or ruination.

Oil refineries were centered in six areas – the producing region in northeast Pennsylvania, Cleveland, Pittsburgh, New York, Philadelphia and Baltimore. Three railroad systems linked these areas. In 1871, Tom Scott, President of the Pennsylvania Railroad, conceived a scheme of secret cooperation among railroads and refiners to end freight rate competition and limit oil refining output. He formed the South Improvement Company (SIC) for this purpose and invited Rockefeller to join. SIC was short lived, but Rockefeller used it as a threat in what became known as the 'Cleveland Massacre' to acquire most of Cleveland's competing refiners, most for less than half of what they felt their business was worth. Within a year most of these refineries were shut down.

The Pennsylvania legislature soon canceled SIC's charter. Oil producers then joined together as a Producers Association, and all significant refiners coalesced into a Refiners Combination headed by Rockefeller.

Agreement was soon reached that that producers sell crude oil only to Combination refiners, and refiners buy crude only from Association producers, at a uniform price to be based on the market price of refined oil. In a separate agreement refiners agreed to take no rebates: Rockefeller was receiving rebates even when he signed this agreement.

It didn't work for long. Members of the Producers Association soon began cheating by exceeding their pumping quotas, and free-riding refiners stayed outside the Combination while still benefiting from the higher price umbrella. Moreover, some Cleveland refiners that Rockefeller had bought built new refineries and re-entered the business.

America went into a depression in 1873, but Standard Oil maintained profitability. Many other refiners went broke. Rockefeller used the opportunity to begin buying up competitors, a practice he continued for several years. Many of these purchases were secret; the companies continued to operate under their pre-sale names.

Early on, Rockefeller saw that shipping oil in barrels was unreasonable; the package cost more than the product. Railroads refused to invest in tank cars, so Standard Oil developed and built its own, which by 1874 they were leasing to the railroads. These made shipping actual barrels prohibitively expensive. For a while, Standard Oil controlled all the tank cars used by Standard and its competitors.

Rockefeller soon controlled most of the refining capacity in Cleveland, Pittsburgh, Philadelphia and New York. Three of the four railroads connecting to the eastern seaboard were tied in with favorable rebate schedules. Only the Baltimore & Ohio Railroad and the West Virginia refineries it served carrying oil to Baltimore for export remained outside of Rockefeller's dominance. But not for long.

In May of 1875 Rockefeller secretly bought J.N. Camden & Company of Parkersburg, West Virginia. Camden then quickly bought up three Parkersburg competitors. Rockefeller/Standard Oil now owned almost all refining capacity in America, and through his arrangements with the railroads he controlled and profited from almost all shipping of crude and refined oil. He knew what and to where his competitors were shipping, at what prices, and he got drawbacks on most of it.

This gave Rockefeller virtual control of the petroleum business, worldwide (except for some wells in Russia, the Pennsylvania oil field was the only one known at the time). But there remained the looming transportation competition – pipelines.

By 1865, Samuel Van Syckel had completed five miles of 2-inch pipe from a well to the railroad, and it worked. That same year, Joseph D. Potts founded the Empire Transportation Company. By the mid-1870s, Empire operated a small fleet of boats carrying grain and produce on the Great Lakes, railroad cars (including 1,500 petroleum tank cars), and 520 miles of oil pipelines. It hauled 3,000,000 barrels of oil annually, mostly from independent oil refiners. And by then it was partially owned by the Pennsylvania Railroad, from which Standard Oil bought Empire Transportation in October 1877.

Standard Oil bought many small pipeline operations soon after they got started. In 1879, Pennsylvania's independent producers succeeded in building their own pipeline, the Tide-Water Pipe Line Company. Rockefeller tried many ways to block its advance to the Atlantic, but without success. But Standard Oil agents were secretly buying Tidewater stock. Rockefeller took control of the company in

1882, bringing virtually all of America's pipelines again under Standard Oil control

In 1880 the *New York World* called Standard Oil "the most cruel, impudent, pitiless, and grasping monopoly that ever fastened upon a country". To critics Rockefeller replied, "In a business so large as ours ... some things are likely to be done which we cannot approve. We correct them as soon as they come to our knowledge."

For years, Standard Oil's opponents sought relief in the courts and state legislatures, with little to show for their efforts. Standard's enormous financial advantage enabled it to usually prevail in court, sometimes by bribing jurors. Standard's 'owned' legislators often blocked legislation. And processes that might lead to unfavorable outcomes (for Standard) were subjected to seemingly endless delays.

Anti-Standard Oil legislation slowly made its way through state and federal legislatures to be signed into law. In response, Standard oil generally made changes to mostly negate the effect of such laws.

Until this time most states did not allow companies incorporated in them to own property in other states, so Standard Oil's acquired companies continued legal existence as separate firms. Its major directors lived in several different cities, making coordinated management difficult. To get around intrastate corporation laws, Standard Oil formed a unique trust arrangement in 1872.

> "you could have a common name, a common office, and a common management by means of a common executive committee. The stock could in effect be made common by placing the corporate stock in the hands of trustees who shall issue certificates of interest in the Trust estate, which certificates will be entitled to their due proportions of the various stock dividends ...

Rockefeller worked to insulate himself from charges brought against Standard oil. He was one of the nine trustees of the Standard

Oil Trust, which met daily over lunch at its New York headquarters. There he functioned through persuasion to achieve consensus on decisions; no policy directions could be directly attributed to him; he was only a trustee with no management control over any Company operation or function.

In 1887 Congress passed the *Interstate Commerce Act*. The law required "just and reasonable" (railroad) rates, and it prohibited special rates or rebates for individual shippers and preference rates for any specific sites, shippers, or products. It established an Interstate Commerce Commission (ICC). The law was not very effective; railroads published rates and conditions available to all, but only Standard Oil had the volume and facilities necessary to earn the most favorable rates. And Standard Oil continued to demand and get preferential treatment that translated to lowered costs in countless other ways.

The Act had little impact on Standard Oil's operations until 1903. In that year it would be amended by the *Elkins Act* to authorize heavy fines on railroads that offer rebates, and upon shippers that accept rebates. *Elkins* would also make railroad corporations, their officers, and their employees liable for discriminatory practices.

By 1887 Standard Oil was functioning as the perfect business Rockefeller had envisioned in 1870, and much of its organization and operations remained a secret from the general public. But as the *Interstate Commerce Act* was being debated in 1887 ...

> The feeling grew all over the country that ... there was danger in the mysterious organization by which such immense fortunes and such excessive power could be built up ... A new trial was coming for Mr. Rockefeller, one much more serious than any trial for overt acts, for the very nature of his great creation was to be in question. It was a hard trial, for all John D. Rockefeller asked of the world by the year 1887 was to be left alone. He had completed one of the most

perfect business organizations the world has ever seen, an organization which handled practically all of a great natural product. His factories were the most perfect and were managed with the strictest economy. He owned outright the pipe-lines which transported the crude oil. His knowledge of the consuming power of the world was accurate, and he kept his output strictly within its limit. At the same time the great marketing machinery he had put in operation carried an aggressive campaign for new markets (all over the world) ...

In the House of Representatives, when the question of ordering an investigation of trusts... was up in 1887, the liveliest concern was shown as to whether the Standard Oil Company ... would escape ... It was certain indeed now that Mr. Rockefeller would not be allowed much longer to work in the dark.

Rockefeller was more than just aware of everything Standard operatives were doing, he was directing and controlling them. And these included a long list of illicit and unethical machinations. But Rockefeller was a pious churchgoer who gave generously to charities, and he treated employees fairly and generously. He seemed blind to these contradictions.

In 1890 opponents of trusts in general and Standard Oil in particular were able to pass the *Sherman Antitrust Act*, which would ultimately be used to end Standard Oil's monopoly. But before that happened, in 1897, Rockefeller retired. He was 58 years old.

In 1906 the U.S. Justice Department sued Standard Oil for multiple violations of the *Sherman Antitrust Act*. In 1911 the U.S. Supreme Court ordered Standard to break into 34 independent companies. John D. Rockefeller owned a quarter of the shares of each of the resultant companies, and those share values mostly doubled. He emerged from the dissolution as the richest man in the world.

John D. Rockefeller was a business genius who contributed mightily to the economic development of America. But he regularly employed unethical practices that were legal at the time, along with practices that were clearly unlawful even then. He was never held accountable in any meaningful way; he might have been had he reported to a truly independent board of directors, and had he and his agents not influenced and bribed so many persons who were in positions to call him to account.

Chapter 6:
Coercion, Predation and Monopoly

Figure 6-1. Standard Oil as portrayed in the September 7, 1904 issue of *Puck* *m*agazine. Painting is by Joseph Keppler, Jr. (Courtesy Wikimedia Commons)

Born July 8, 1839, on a rude homestead near the little town of Richford in upstate New York, John Davison Rockefeller was the second child and first son of William and Eliza Rockefeller. He would have four sisters and a brother, plus two half-sisters born of the family's housekeeper.

His father, a shady character variously known as "Devil Bill" and other aliases, moved the family frequently and was away far more than he was home. Nevertheless, while they were living in Moravia, New York, John learned a great deal about practical business from his father.

> When it came to business ethics, Bill was a most curious compound, extremely honorable one moment, a sharpster the next. To his son he tacitly conveyed the message that commerce was a tough, competitive struggle and that you were entitled to outwit the other fellow by any means, fair or foul. He tutored John in a sharp, relentless bargaining style ...[a]

John loved detail and had a natural affinity for numbers. He also developed a love of money, and a firm attachment to the Baptist church.

The family moved to Owego, New York in 1850. Two years later John entered Owego Academy, where he obtained an excellent secondary-school education. By 1854 the family had relocated to Cleveland, Ohio, where he completed a three-month course at a business college. There he learned bookkeeping, which he soon viewed as crucial for success in business, and fundamental principals of business transactions.

Upon graduation, at the age of 16, Rockefeller set out to find his first regular job. He targeted the waterfront area teeming with lumber mills, iron foundries, warehouses and shipyards.

> I tramped the streets for days and weeks, asking merchants and storekeepers if they didn't want a boy; but the offer of my services met with little appreciation. No one wanted a boy ... At last one man on the Cleveland docks told me that I might come back after the noonday meal ...
>
> "We will give you a chance," he said ... This was September 26, 1855 ...[b]

The firm was Hewitt and Tuttle, commission merchants and produce shippers. Rockefeller kept books, wrote letters, paid bills and collected receivables. When Tuttle left the firm in early 1857,

---

[a] *TITAN, The Life of John D. Rockefeller, Sr.*, Chapter 2, Ron Chernow.
[b] *Random Reminiscences of Men and Events*, Chapter 2, John D. Rockefeller.

Rockefeller was promoted to chief bookkeeper and given all of Tuttle's responsibilities, but at only one-quarter the pay. Rockefeller didn't stay long.

With savings and a loan from his father, on April 1, 1858, John and his friend Maurice B. Clark became partners in Clark and Rockefeller, a new commission house that traded in commodities shipping through the port of Cleveland. They were successful, but a discovery less than 100 miles east would soon change the partners' lives and lead to John D. Rockefeller becoming the wealthiest American in history.

Prior to 1859 whale-oil and camphene lamps were the most modern artificial lighting in homes and businesses throughout the world. Oil for such lamps was also made from other sources; several companies in Cleveland, for instance, were refining "coal oil" from bituminous coal. But the Civil War cut off the supply of southern turpentine, from which camphene was made, and it disrupted the whaling industry. Prices for illuminating oils doubled.

Petroleum, then called rock oil, had been in sparing use for many years in applications ranging from patent medicines to cosmetics to lubricants, but it was available only in small amounts mostly skimmed off surfaces of ponds and creeks. However, in 1855, Yale Professor Benjamin Silliman reported that a high-quality illuminating oil – kerosene – could be refined from this oil. So some began digging wells in search of the sources of the rock oil that seeped up through the ground.

On August 27, 1859, Edwin Drake struck oil at 69 feet below ground near Titusville, Pennsylvania. An oil rush ensued. Soon many wells in the area were producing oil – a few thousand barrels[a] even during the remainder of 1859. In just 14 years annual production would reach 10 million barrels, and northwestern Pennsylvania would be producing virtually all of the world's petroleum-based oil.

---

[a]   One "barrel" of crude oil equals 42 U.S. gallons.

Figure 6-2. Edwin Drake's well.

Rockefeller didn't join the oil rush. But within a few years he entered the oil business, not as a producer at the wells, but downstream as a refiner. He was drawn into the business through Maurice Clark's friendship with Samuel Andrews;

> Andrews was a self-taught chemist, a born tinkerer, and an enterprising mechanic. Arriving in Cleveland in the 1850s, he worked in a lard-oil refinery owned by ... C.A. Dean, and acquired extensive experience in making tallow, candles and coal oil. Then, in 1860, Dean got a ten-barrel shipment of Pennsylvania crude from which Andrews distilled the first oil-based kerosene manufactured in Cleveland ...
>
> An expert on illuminants enthralled by the unique properties of kerosene, Andrews was convinced it would outshine and outsell other sources of light ... by 1862 Sam was plotting to leave Dean and strike out on his own. On the lookout for backers, he frequently stopped by the offices of Clark and Rockefeller ...
>
> Rockefeller and Maurice Clark pledged $4,000 for half the working capital of the new refining venture, Andrews,

Clark and Co., placing the twenty-year-old Rockefeller squarely in the oil business in 1863[a]

Andrews, Clark and Co. erected its new refinery just a mile and a half east of downtown Cleveland on Kingston Run. This narrow access to the Cuyahoga River and, thus, to Lake Erie, soon hosted a string of competing refineries.

Rockefeller spent many hours at the refinery "going to the cooper shop to roll out barrels, stack hoops, or cart out shavings."[b] But Rockefeller and the Clark brothers didn't get along so, in early 1865, Rockefeller bought out their interest and partnered with Sam Andrews. Their refinery was, by then, the largest in Cleveland.

Henry M. Flagler joined the partnership in 1867. The next year he brokered a secret deal with railroads that rebated 71% of published freight rates in return for a promise to load, ship and unload at least 60 carloads of oil per day. Railroads had long been allowing such volume-discount rebates[c] on shipments of other commodities, but Rockefeller, Andrews and Flagler was the only oil refiner then able to guarantee such volumes.

By the late 1860s the oil industry was plagued by rampant over-production, which pushed prices so low that many or most producers and refiners were unprofitable. Freight rebates helped the Partnership to reduce its kerosene price from 58 cents/gallon in 1865 to 26 cents/gallon by 1870. But Rockefeller saw his success as a refiner

---

[a] *TITAN, The Life of John D. Rockefeller, Sr.*, Chapter 5, Ron Chernow.

[b] Ibid.

[c] Rebating off published prices for rail shipments was an established practice well before petroleum became a significant commodity. Cleveland was serviced by three railroads, and by water transportation via the Great Lakes and via the Erie Canal to the Hudson River. However, crude oil had to be shipped overland to Cleveland from the Pennsylvania oil fields.

threatened, and he decided that industry conditions called for consolidation and cooperation to limit supply and sustain prices.

> Rockefeller cited the years 1869 and 1870 as the start of his campaign to replace competition with cooperation in the industry. The culprit, he decided, was "over-development of the refining industry," which created "ruinous competition" ... he began to envision a giant cartel that would reduce overcapacity, stabilize prices, and rationalize the industry.[a]

On January 10, 1870 Rockefeller, Andrews and Flagler was superseded by the Standard Oil Company (Ohio), a joint-stock firm with John D. Rockefeller as President, his brother William as Vice President, and Henry M. Flagler as Secretary and Treasurer.

Rockefeller had tried to get producers to curtail output, but this approach never worked. There were too many producers and more wells coming on line almost every day; they had to keep pumping crude to service their loans, regardless of profitability. Though Standard Oil remained profitable, Rockefeller estimated, in 1870, that 90 per cent of all refineries were losing money.

All crude had to pass through refineries and be transported to market. Rockefeller saw that he could control supply and pricing of both crude (buyers' market) and refined products (sellers' market) if he could consolidate refining capacity. Such consolidation would enable continuing favorable transportation arrangements with railroads, both asymmetrical rebates and drawbacks[b]. Attendant scale economies in refined products would enable lower prices for consumer sales, and for squeezing competitors targeted for agreement, acquisition or ruination.

Oil refineries were centered in six areas – the producing region in northeast Pennsylvania, Cleveland, Pittsburgh, New York, Philadelphia

---

[a]   *TITAN, The Life of John D. Rockefeller, Sr.*, Chapter 8, Ron Chernow.
[b]   Railroads paid Standard Oil a portion of freight charges billed to Standard's competitors!

and Baltimore. Three railroad systems linked these areas – the Erie, the New York Central and the Pennsylvania. In 1871, Tom Scott, President of the Pennsylvania Railroad, conceived a scheme of secret cooperation among the railroads and refiners to end freight rate competition and limit oil refining output. He formed the South Improvement Company (SIC) for this purpose and, because Standard Oil was then the largest refiner, invited Rockefeller to join. While SIC was short lived, and never did any actual business, Rockefeller used it as a threat in what became known as the 'Cleveland Massacre.'

> It was on the second of January, 1872, that the organisation of the South Improvement Company was completed. ... There were at that time some twenty-six refineries in the town, some of them very large plants. ... To the owners of these refineries Mr. Rockefeller now went one by one, and explained the South Improvement Company. "You see," he told them, "this scheme is bound to work. It means an absolute control by us of the oil business. There is no chance for anyone outside. But we are going to give everybody a chance to come in. You are to turn over your refinery to my appraisers, and I will give you Standard Oil Company stock or cash, as you prefer, for the value we put upon it." ... It was useless to resist (Rockefeller) told the hesitating; they would certainly be crushed if they did not accept his offer ...
>
> Under the combined threat and persuasion of the Standard ...almost the entire independent oil interest of Cleveland collapsed ... From a capacity of probably not over 1,500 barrels of crude a day, the Standard Oil Company rose in three months' time to one of 10,000 barrels. ... it became master of over one-fifth of the refining capacity of the United States ...[a]

At least 21 refiners sold out, most for less than half of what they felt their business was worth. Those who accepted Standard Oil Stock

---

[a] *The History of the Standard Oil Company*, briefer version, Chapter 2, Ida M. Tarbell, Edited by David M. Chalmers.

would become quite wealthy; those who demanded cash would forever feel cheated. Within a year most of these refineries were shut down.

Oil region producers and refiners soon learned about the arrangements between SIC and Standard Oil. Their outrage quickly escalated into the 'Oil War of 1872', which lasted until year end.

> Amid this frenzied hue and cry, the local citizenry created a small army of roving protesters ... On the night of March 1, refiners and producers jammed another tumultuous meeting ... in Oil City. One featured speaker ... supported a proposal ... to cut existing production by 30 percent and suspend new drilling for 30 days ... By the end of the meeting, a thousand men stood ready to besiege the state capitol in Harrisburg and demand relief from the SIC ...
>
> In this warlike atmosphere ... Saboteurs attacked the railroads, raiding oil cars and spilling their contents on the ground or tearing tracks apart ... Few residents of Oil Creek imagined that their dread adversary was a clean-cut, churchgoing young man ...
>
> Far from giving Rockefeller pause, the vandalism only confirmed his view of Oil Creek as a netherworld of rogues and adventurers who needed to be ruled by stronger men. He was always quick to impugn the motives of enemies while regarding his own as somehow beyond reproach.[a]

The Pennsylvania legislature canceled SIC's charter in April. Oil producers joined together as a Producers Association, and all significant refiners coalesced into a Refiners Combination (the 'Pittsburgh Plan') headed by Rockefeller.

The Producers Association was able to shut off virtually all production for 30 days, but Rockefeller gave them an offer they couldn't refuse, to purchase 200,000 barrels of crude. Agreement was soon reached. It anticipated that all producers be part of the Association and all refiners be part of the Combination. It stipulated

---

[a]   *TITAN, The Life of John D. Rockefeller, Sr.*, Chapter 8, Ron Chernow.

that producers sell crude oil only to Combination refiners, and refiners buy crude only from Association producers, at a uniform price to be based on the market price of refined oil. In a separate agreement refiners agreed to "take no rebates ... As we now know, Mr. Rockefeller himself was receiving rebates when he signed this agreement."[a]

It didn't work for long. Members of the Producers Association soon began cheating by exceeding their pumping quotas, and free-riding refiners stayed outside the Combination while still benefiting from the higher price umbrella. Moreover, some Cleveland refiners that Rockefeller had bought built new refineries and re-entered the business.

> Rockefeller had clarified one thing in his own mind ... Voluntary associations couldn't move with the speed, unity, and efficiency he wanted ... He was now through with ineffectual alliances and ready to bring the industry to heel under Standard Oil control ...
>
> In the end, frustrated by rampant cheating and freeloaders, Rockefeller gathered refiners in Sarasota Springs, New York, on June 24. 1873, and dissolved the short-lived Pittsburgh Plan.[b]

America went into a depression in 1873, but Standard Oil maintained profitability. Many other refiners went broke. Rockefeller used the opportunity to begin buying up competitors, a practice he continued for several years. Many of these purchases were secret; the companies continued to operate under their pre-sale names. Their former owners, now Standard Oil employees, managed them as Standard Oil directed.

[a] *The History of the Standard Oil Company*, briefer version, Chapter 4, Ida M. Tarbell, Edited by David M. Chalmers.
[b] *TITAN, The Life of John D. Rockefeller, Sr.*, Chapter 9, Ron Chernow.

> Rockefeller was capable of extraordinary ferocity in compelling submission from competitors. He might starve out obdurate firms by buying all available barrels on the market or monopolize local tank cars to paralyze their operations. Yet ... Rockefeller preferred patience and reason – if possible – to terror. He was not only purchasing refineries but assembling a management team. The creation of Standard Oil was often less a matter of stamping out competitors than of seducing them into cooperation.[a]

In 1874 Rockefeller began to bring more refiners into Standard Oil. In June, he and Flagler met secretly with the largest refiners in Pittsburgh and Philadelphia to persuade them to come into the Company. After examining the Standard Oil financial records and seeing that Standard could make a profit selling kerosene at a price lower than their costs, they agreed to join. Charles Lockhart and William G. Warden traded their companies for Standard Oil stock and became important members of Standard Oil's management team (secretly, for several years).

With these two acquisitions, Rockefeller got a significant part of the refining capacity in these two refining areas. Lockhart and Warden then spearheaded consolidation of competitive refineries in their areas; by 1876 only one of the 24 Pittsburgh refineries remained in independent business.

Even before wrapping up in Pittsburgh and Philadelphia, Rockefeller began a similar campaign in New York. Standard Oil had already acquired two major New York firms – Devoe Manufacturing, which made lubricants, and the Long Island Company, a large refinery. But the key acquisition was Charles Pratt and Company; Charles Pratt not only had a popular kerosene brand with European distribution, he was a brilliant businessman who enthusiastically joined the Standard

---

[a]   Ibid.

Oil team. (He would become disenchanted and leave the Company in the 1880s).

With the Pratt acquisition came Henry H. Rogers who would become one of Standard Oil's top executives. He would, over time, direct the Company's crude-oil purchases and the developing pipelines and manufacturing operations.

Early on, Rockefeller saw that shipping oil in barrels was unreasonable; the package cost more than the product. He had tried to persuade the railroads to invest in tank cars to carry crude. They weren't interested, so Standard Oil developed and built tank cars, which by 1874 they were leasing to the railroads. These made shipping actual barrels prohibitively expensive. For a while, Standard Oil controlled all the tank cars used by Standard and its competitors.

By now a pattern with Rockefeller, he began to squeeze competing New York refiners.

> New York Independents began to experience unaccountable shortages of vital supplies. John Ellis and Company, which manufactured petroleum jelly, suddenly found it couldn't book the requisite railroad cars for crude-oil shipments. Some invisible force was working against them. As the firm tried to unravel this mystery, a Standard Oil representative took the opportunity to drop by for a friendly chat with John Ellis and warned him, "You are helpless. You will have to sell out" ... Ellis stayed independent, but few firms had the resources or fortitude to withstand the unceasing pressure exerted by the growing legions of Standard Oil minions.[a]

Rockefeller now controlled most of the refining capacity in Cleveland, Pittsburgh, Philadelphia and New York. Three of the four railroads connecting to the eastern seaboard were tied in with favorable rebate schedules. Only the Baltimore & Ohio Railroad and

------

[a]   Ibid.

the West Virginia refineries it served carrying oil to Baltimore for export remained outside of Rockefeller's dominance. But not for long.

In May of 1875 Rockefeller secretly bought J.N. Camden & Company of Parkersburg, West Virginia. At about the same time, thinking it was aiding independents in their struggle with Standard Oil, the B&O gave Camden favorable rebates plus a drawback of $.10 per barrel on all refined oil shipped by Camden *and* its perceived competitors including Standard Oil. Camden then quickly bought up three Parkersburg competitors.

Rockefeller/Standard Oil now owned almost all refining capacity in America, and through his arrangements with the railroads he controlled and profited from almost all shipping of crude and refined oil. He knew what and to where his competitors were shipping, at what prices, and he got drawbacks on most of it.

This gave Rockefeller virtual control of the petroleum business, worldwide (except for some wells in Russia, the Pennsylvania oil field was the only one known at the time). But there remained the Oil City refineries and looming transportation competition – pipelines.

That oil could be moved by pipeline over short distances from oil field to local refineries and shipping points was demonstrated in the 1860s, but the first few attempts leaked great amounts of oil and failed commercially. Then, in 1865, Samuel Van Syckel completed five miles of 2-inch pipe from a well to the railroad, and it worked! It was, according to Ida Tarbell, the second most important event in the history of Pennsylvania's oil region.

That same year, Joseph D. Potts founded the Empire Transportation Company. By the mid-1870s, Empire operated a small fleet of boats carrying grain and produce on the Great Lakes, railroad cars (including 1,500 petroleum tank cars), and 520 miles of oil pipelines. It hauled 3,000,000 barrels of oil annually, mostly from independent oil refiners. And by then it was partially owned by the Pennsylvania Railroad.

In 1877, Potts expanded into oil refining. Rockefeller objected to Tom Scott of the Pennsylvania Railroad. As part of the ensuing 'negotiation', Standard Oil shut down its Pittsburgh refineries, depriving the Railroad of 65 percent of its oil traffic. Scott capitulated; Standard Oil bought Empire Transportation in October 1877.

Standard Oil bought many small pipeline operations soon after they got started. In 1879, Pennsylvania's independent producers succeeded in building their own pipeline, the Tide-Water Pipe Line Company. Rockefeller tried many ways to block its advance to the Atlantic, but without success. Tidewater completed a 6-inch line to the Bayonne, New Jersey refineries in just three months. But Standard Oil agents were secretly buying Tidewater stock. Rockefeller took control of the company in 1882, bringing virtually all of America's pipelines again under Standard Oil control.

In 1880 the *New York World* called Standard Oil "the most cruel, impudent, pitiless, and grasping monopoly that ever fastened upon a country". To critics Rockefeller replied, "In a business so large as ours ... some things are likely to be done which we cannot approve. We correct them as soon as they come to our knowledge."[a]

For years, Standard Oil's opponents sought relief in the courts and state legislatures, with little to show for their efforts. Rockefeller used Standard's enormous financial advantage enabled it to usually prevail in court, sometimes by bribing jurors. Standard's 'owned' legislators often blocked legislation. And processes that might lead to unfavorable outcomes (for Standard) were subjected to seemingly endless delays.

---

[a] *John D. Rockefeller: Anointed With Oil*, Grant Segal.

Anti-Standard Oil legislation slowly made its way through state and federal legislatures to be signed into law. In response, Standard oil generally made changes to mostly negate the effect of such laws.

As noted, in April 1872 Pennsylvania canceled the SIC Charter before related business was even begun. Rockefeller reacted, and perhaps anticipated the action, by building a monopoly through ownership that superseded cooperative approaches.

At this time most states did not allow companies incorporated in them to own property in other states, so Standard Oil's acquired companies continued legal existence as separate firms in separate states. Thus, its major directors lived in several different cities, making coordinated management difficult. To get around intrastate corporation laws, Standard Oil formed a unique trust arrangement in 1872.

> The answer … was that "you could have a common name, a common office, and a common management by means of a common executive committee. The stock could in effect be made common by placing the corporate stock in the hands of trustees who shall issue certificates of interest in the Trust estate, which certificates will be entitled to their due proportions of the various stock dividends … this elaborate stock swap would create a union not of corporations but of stockholders, ensuring that the companies could behave in concert without running afoul of the law.[a]

Rockefeller worked to insulate himself from charges brought against Standard oil. He was one trustee of the Standard Oil Trust, which met daily over lunch at its New York headquarters. There he functioned through persuasion to achieve consensus on decisions; no policy directions could be directly attributed to him; he did not even sit at the head of the 'luncheon' table. Rockefeller was only a trustee with no management control over any Company operation or function.

---

[a]   *TITAN, The Life of John D. Rockefeller, Sr.,* Chapter 13, Ron Chernow.

(There were nine equal trustees, but one was certainly more equal than the others!)

In 1887 Congress passed the *Interstate Commerce Act*. The new law required "just and reasonable" (railroad) rates, and it prohibited special rates or rebates for individual shippers and preference rates for any specific sites, shippers, or products. It established an Interstate Commerce Commission (ICC). The law was not very effective; railroads published rates and conditions available to all, but only Standard Oil had the volume and facilities necessary to earn the most favorable rates. And Standard Oil continued to demand and get preferential treatment that translated to lowered costs in countless other ways.

The Act had little impact on Standard oil's operations until 1903. In that year it would be amended by the *Elkins Act* to authorize heavy fines on railroads that offer rebates, and upon shippers that accept rebates. *Elkins* would also make railroad corporations, their officers, and their employees liable for discriminatory practices. In 1906 the *Hepburn Act* would extend ICC effective authority over more of Standard Oil's operations including terminals and pipelines.

By 1887 Standard Oil was functioning as the perfect business Rockefeller had envisioned in 1870, and much of its organization and operations remained a secret from the general public. But as the *Interstate Commerce Act* was being debated in 1887 …

> The feeling grew all over the country that … there was danger in the mysterious organization by which such immense fortunes and such excessive power could be built up on one side of an industry, while another side steadily lost money and power. A new trial was coming for Mr. Rockefeller, one much more serious than any trial for overt acts, for the very nature of his great creation was to be in question. It was a hard trial, for all John D. Rockefeller asked of the world by the year 1887 was to be left alone. He

had completed one of the most perfect business organizations the world has ever seen, an organization which handled practically all of a great natural product. His factories were the most perfect and were managed with the strictest economy. He owned outright the pipe-lines which transported the crude oil. His knowledge of the consuming power of the world was accurate, and he kept his output strictly within its limit. At the same time the great marketing machinery he had put in operation carried an aggressive campaign for new markets (all over the world) ... The Standard Oil Company had been organized to do business, and if ever a company did business it was this one ...

The feeling grew that the Standard Oil Company, or Trust, as it was by this time generally called, must be looked into ... In the House of Representatives, when the question of ordering an investigation of trusts... was up in 1887, the liveliest concern was shown as to whether the Standard Oil Company ... would escape ... The same interest was shown in the Senate of New York State, where an investigation was ordered for February, 1888. It was certain indeed now that Mr. Rockefeller would not be allowed much longer to work in the dark.[a]

Rockefeller was more than just aware of everything Standard operatives were doing, he was directing and controlling them. And these included a long list of illicit and unethical machinations. But Rockefeller was a pious churchgoer who gave generously to charities (he would later become known for that aspect of his personality), and he treated employees fairly and generously. He seemed blind to these contradictions.

In 1890 opponents of trusts in general and Standard Oil in particular were able to pass the *Sherman Antitrust Act*. While it would ultimately be used to end Standard Oil's monopoly, it had little immediate impact on Company operations.

---

[a] *The History of the Standard Oil Company,* briefer version, Chapter 13, Ida M. Tarbell, Edited by David M. Chalmers.

After more than two decades building Standard Oil, Rockefeller was weary. He yearned for retirement and began withdrawing from day-to-day operations in 1894 or 1895. By the time he was 58 years old, in 1897, he was retired completely.

Epilogue

John D. Rockefeller was not brought to account for misdeeds of the Standard Oil Company. Indeed, he became the world's wealthiest man after he retired!

> As Rockefeller moved into retirement, his wealth was accumulating at an astonishing rate. During his tenure at Standard Oil, the trust had usually paid a fixed dividend of 12 percent, reflecting his prudent leadership. With Archibald at the helm, by contrast, the dividends surged, jumping to 31 percent in 1896 and 33 percent in 1897 and 1899. Buoyed by these dividends, the price of Standard Oil shares leaped from 176 in 1896 to 458 three years later. However much Rockefeller deplored this extravagant dividend policy, he was its foremost beneficiary ...[a]

In 1906 the U.S. Justice Department sued Standard Oil for multiple violations of the *Sherman Antitrust Act* during the preceding four years. The court verdict was that Standard Oil was an unreasonable monopoly and should be broken up. In 1911 the U.S. Supreme Court agreed and ordered Standard to break into 34 independent companies. (Today, the major successor companies are ExxonMobil, Chevron, Marathon Petroleum, and BP.) John D. Rockefeller owned a quarter of the shares of each of the resultant companies, and those share values mostly doubled. He emerged from the dissolution as the richest man in the world.

---

[a]   *TITAN, The Life of John D. Rockefeller, Sr.*, Chapter 20, Ron Chernow.

From very early in life Rockefeller gave significantly to charity. By the time he was twenty, his charity exceeded ten percent of his income. As Rockefeller's wealth grew, so did his giving, primarily to educational and public health causes, but also for basic science and the arts. He came to believe that charitable giving should be managed like a business; he established the forerunner of the Rockefeller Foundation charitable trust in 1891. Rockefeller provided major funding for what became Spelman College, and he gave $80 million to the University of Chicago, turning a small Baptist college into a world-class institution. Rockefeller was also a significant contributor to established institutions including Columbia, Brown, Harvard, Vassar and Yale. His Rockefeller Foundation, which focused on public health, medical training, and the arts, endowed Johns Hopkins School of Hygiene and Public Health. During his lifetime, Rockefeller donated more than a half-billion dollars to charity.

John Davison Rockefeller died May 23, 1937 at age 97.

Chapter 7:
Analysis and Discussion – John D. Rockefeller/ Standard Oil Company

Once he was in the oil business, John D. Rockefeller was a visionary. Repeatedly, he appraised situations, saw what he must do to profit in the long run, and proceeded to do it. Not many laws of the time restricted his actions; when he encountered ones that did he found ways to get around them, some of them extralegal and not directly linked to him. He was smarter than most opponents, always ahead of them mentally.

Rockefeller was at the top of the Standard Oil corporate hierarchy, minimizing structural accountability. He also worked to gain consensus on major company decisions to diffuse apparent accountability. He routinely used proxies in secret to deflect attention from himself. And he was a master of obfuscation when people tried to pin him down.

Rockefeller avoided a personal paper trail – written and personal directives – concerning Standard Oil activities. Thus, he was usually able to claim ignorance of nefarious activities; he had plausible deniability.

He was virtually free of all structural, legal and civil accountability. Consider that most of the six critical accountability conditions were absent in John D. Rockefeller's actions related to Standard Oil.

1. Once he was running his own company, the scope of Rockefeller's responsibilities was not articulated by any other person or agency. This is often the case when the top executive

is also the founder or owner. But when Rockefeller was charged by legal or public entities with responsibility for specific acts of company employees or agents, he would deny knowledge of the act and, by implication, deny responsibility.

2. There was no personal superior-subordinate relationship. Rockefeller was virtually always 'the boss.'

3. There was no one-to-one superior-subordinate relationship. Rockefeller was usually just one among several or many equal votes. (Of course, his vote was "more equal" than others.)

5. Rockefeller wielded substantial control or influence, most of it financial, over people to whom he was nominally accountable.

6. No one individual had authority to censure, restrain or otherwise significantly affect Rockefeller; he was independently wealthy.

Conclusions

John D. Rockefeller was a business genius. He contributed mightily to the economic development of America. But he regularly employed unethical practices that were legal at the time, and practices that were unlawful even then. He was never held accountable in any meaningful way, though he might have been had he reported to a truly independent board of directors, and had he and his agents not influenced and bribed so many persons who were in positions to call him to account. He always maintained 'plausible deniability' concerning actions that might otherwise be attributed to him.

Questions to Consider

- Suppose business laws had required complete ownership transparency, and had been enforced. How might that have reduced chicanery in Standard Oil's dealings? Historically, what might have changed?
- Standard Oil's directors were all "inside" men. Would accountability have been improved if most of them had been "outside" directors?
- Standard Oil's stock was very closely held (by just a few families). Suppose it had been widely held (by thousands of shareholders). How might this have affected accountability?
- Relevant laws have changed much since the time of Rockefeller. Do you believe he could have built an economic organization like Standard Oil today? Why or why not?

Chapter 8:
Additional Reading – John D. Rockefeller/ Standard Oil Company

Chernow, Ron. *TITAN The Life of John D. Rockefeller, Sr.* Second Edition. Vintage Books, March 2004.

Rockefeller, John D. *Random Reminiscences of Men and Events.* Compass Circle, 2019.

Segall, Grant. *John D. Rockefeller: Anointed With Oil.* Oxford University Press, 2001.

Tarbell, Ida M. *The History of the Standard Oil Company;* Briefer Version edited by David M. Chalmers. DOVER Publications 2003.

Also, search the internet for topics such as: Standard Oil, Standard Oil Company, John D. Rockefeller, etc.

Case 3:

Ralph J. Cordiner/General Electric Company

Chapter 9:
Executive Summary

After devising a commercially viable electric light bulb, Thomas A. Edison set out to create an electric utility to compete with existing gas light utilities. In December 1880, he founded the Edison Illuminating Company. In 1892 Edison General Electric merged with competitor Thomson-Houston. The newly formed General Electric Company controlled three-quarters of the U.S. electrical business, and would strengthen its position through acquisition of many smaller companies over the next decades.

Ralph J. Cordiner was born March 20, 1900. The Cordiners lived on the family wheat farm north of Walla Walla, Washington. Cordiner graduated from High School in 1917, and immediately joined the Navy. He was soon selected for Officer Candidate School, but World War I ended before he was commissioned.

Cordiner then enrolled in Whitman College, where he majored in economics. He graduated in 1922. Later that year Cordiner joined the Edison General Electric Appliance Company, in Portland, Oregon.

He became sales manager of G-E Appliances' northwest region in 1927 and, in 1930, its Pacific Coast area. After ten years in field sales, Cordiner was promoted to Manager of Heating Devices in the Appliance and Merchandise Division. He moved to Bridgeport, Connecticut, where the division was headquartered. There he became a protégé of Charles E. Wilson, Division Manager and Vice President. In 1935, Cordiner was promoted to Assistant Division Manager.

When Wilson became Executive Vice President of General Electric in 1938, Cordiner succeeded him as head of the Appliance and Merchandise Division.

Wilson was President of General Electric from 1939 to 1942. He left General Electric to become vice-president of the War Production Board (WPB). Cordiner joined him there as Director General of War Production Scheduling.

Wilson returned to General Electric in 1945 and brought Cordiner along as his assistant. Cordiner was made a Vice President and, in 1949, elevated to the board of directors as Executive Vice President.

General Electric was involved in 11 antitrust suits from 1911 through 1945. In 1946, as a response to these suits, GE formulated a corporate directive that stated it "is the policy of this company to conform to the antitrust laws." Directive Policy 20.5 was repeatedly revised until it eventually read (in part): "It is the policy of the company to comply strictly in all respects with the antitrust laws. There shall be no exception to this policy … ."

Every manager was periodically asked to indicate in writing that he was adhering to the policy. In 1949, three General Electric employees engaged in price-fixing acrobatics were quietly eased out by Cordiner.

In 1950, Cordiner became President and functioned as chief operating officer. In 1958, Cordiner became Chairman of the Board and Chief Executive Officer.

Between 1950 and 1954 Cordiner devoted himself to reinventing the General Electric organization. He believed that GE had become too big to react quickly to changes in the diverse markets it served. Cordiner's ideas were well established by 1953.

Cordiner saw General Electric as tightly tied to the phenomenal growth of electricity in the United States and world wide. He visualized a "benign circle of electric power," and he viewed General Electric as being or becoming the leading supplier of manufactured products to virtually all the markets in this 'circle of electric power' – managed by professional managers for maximum profit.

To achieve and maintain that position, he developed a radically different decentralized organization concept of around 100 'product departments' to develop, produce and market products to specific markets. Each product department was to function as an almost-autonomous business, under a General Manager responsible for maximizing profits over the long run; Cordiner emphasized that "The price of a product can be raised or lowered by the managers of the Department producing it."

Departments serving similar market areas (e.g., consumer, defense, federal government, industrial, utility, etc.) plus a number of sales and service departments were placed in 21 Divisions reporting to seven Executive ("Group") Vice Presidents.

Group Vice Presidents were members of the Executive Office at corporate headquarters, and each Executive Vice President served as the president in a defined Operating area without, in any sense, relieving the corporate president of the ultimate responsibility placed upon him by the Board of Directors.

In early 1959, the Tennessee Valley Authority's frustration over years of identical bids from electrical manufacturers gained the attention of the press, then the Kefauver Antitrust Subcommittee of the Senate and the Antitrust Division of the Department of Justice. It became the biggest price-fixing investigation in U.S. history.

In mid-February, 1960, the grand juries handed down the first of 20 true bills indicting 29 manufacturers and 45 of their officials of colluding to fix prices of electrical apparatus in violation of the *Sherman Antitrust Act*. General Electric was named as a co-conspirator in 19 of the true bills.

All defendants ultimately pleaded guilty or *nolo contendere*. General Electric was fined a total of $407,500 on 19 counts. Seven corporate executives, including two from GE, served short jail sentences; 23 others, including eight from GE, got suspended jail sentences. All 45 individual defendants, 19 of them G-E personnel, were assessed fines ranging from $1,000 to $7,000.

But the matter didn't end there. The Kefauver hearings with public testimony went on for more than two years, during which time witnesses testified to the depth and breadth of the conspiracy.

Corporate representatives had been holding regular price meetings for many years, even back to 1946. They included informal and formal talks and agreements over prices and allocations of business for specific products and product categories. They included agreements as to which company was to be awarded each job put out for bid, with secret formulas to determine the prices that each company would bid to secure that end. Nothing was ever put in writing.

Witnesses before the Kefauver subcommittee confirmed, in effect, all the charges. In addition to fines assessed in 1960, General Electric ultimately paid many millions of dollars in civil suits and, in a 1962 consent decree promised to never do it again.

At General Electric's 1961 annual meeting Cordiner was reelected Chairman of the Board and President.

Cordiner was never held personally accountable for any of these crimes; he never paid any restitution or suffered any personal consequences. But did he know? Or tacitly condone? Or, in the past, even participate? Cordiner repeatedly denied any knowledge of these illegal activities.

Cordiner clearly knew that General Electric had engaged in price fixing and other antitrust activities in the past. It may reasonably be inferred that he was aware of price-fixing in the present. Even if he didn't know, he should have. Cordiner might have been held accountable had he not been a member of the board to which he nominally reported.

Ralph J. Cordiner died on December 5, 1963.

Chapter 10:
Plausible Deniability

Thomas Edison et al formed General Electric to commercialize Edison's patents. That was preceded by his establishing an industrial research lab at Menlo Park, New Jersey, in 1876. Edison's name is registered on more than 1,000 patents ensuing from the lab's work. He formed the Edison Electric Light Company in New York City in 1878.

The incandescent light bulb was not Edison's first patent but, by 1879 when it was filed, it was his most significant. He made the first public demonstration of his light bulb on December 31, 1879, in Menlo Park.

After devising a commercially viable electric light bulb Edison set out to create an electric utility to compete with existing gas light utilities. In December 1880, he founded the Edison Illuminating Company and patented a direct-current (DC) system for electricity distribution in the 1880s. In 1882, Edison's utility began delivering electricity to 59 customers in New York City.

As Edison expanded his DC systems, he began to encounter competition from George Westinghouse and others who were installing alternating-current (AC) systems. As the 'War of Currents' raged on, Edison Illuminating lost ground, and profits dwindled.

The War of Currents ended in 1892 with Edison's being forced out of controlling his own company. That year, Edison General Electric merged with AC competitor Thomson-Houston. The newly formed General Electric Company controlled three-quarters of the U.S. electrical business, and would strengthen its position through acquisition of many smaller companies over the next decades.

In 1893, General Electric bought the business of Rudolf Eickemeyer and its transformers for use in transmission of electrical power. Engineer George Steinmetz came with the acquisition; he soon became known as the engineering wizard of General Electric.

General Electric Consumer Products was founded in 1905 to develop and acquire products for the home. It began marketing a broad line of heating and cooking products in 1907. It would be combined in 1930 with G-E Industrial Systems to form G-E Consumer & Industrial.

General Electric acquired the Hotpoint Electric Heating Company in 1918 and merged it with the Heating Device Section of General Electric. This would become the Edison General Electric Appliance Company and then, in 1931, the Edison General Electric Company.

In 1911, General Electric absorbed the National Electric Lamp Association into its lighting business and established the lighting division headquarters at Nela Park, near Cleveland.

General Electric founded Radio Corporation of America (RCA) in 1919 to market radios to consumers. In 1926, RCA founded the National Broadcasting Company (NBC), which built two radio broadcasting networks. In 1930, General Electric was charged with antitrust violations and was ordered to divest RCA. (GE would re-acquire RCA in 1985.)

General Electric demonstrated television in 1927, and made the first public broadcast in 1929. These developments would evolve into GE's ownership of many radio and television broadcasting stations.

Ralph J.[a] Cordiner was born March 20, 1900. He was the second of four children born to George M. and Mary Jarron Cordiner. The Cordiners lived on the family wheat farm north of Walla Walla, Washington. Cordiner graduated from High School in 1917, and immediately joined the Navy. He was soon selected for Officer

---

[a] 'Jesse' was the middle name given at birth and used throughout Cordiner's school years. At some point, he adopted 'Jarron' as his middle name.

Candidate School, but World War I ended before he was commissioned.

Cordiner then enrolled in Whitman College, where he majored in economics. The 1921-22 Whitman yearbook lists his participation in many school activities including leadership positions on several. He was a member of Phi Delta Theta fraternity, a member of the Whitman College debate team and a member of Delta Sigma Rho (national public-speaking honor society). He graduated in 1922.

While in college Cordiner worked part time to help put himself through school. One of his jobs was with Pacific Power and Light as a salesman of electrical appliances. Upon graduation he stayed on with PP&L as Commercial Manager in Walla Walla.

Later in 1922, Cordiner joined the Edison General Electric Appliance Company, in Portland, Oregon. Cordiner "celebrated his new job by marrying his college sweetheart, Gwyneth (A.) Lewis."[a] They would have four children (all daughters).

He became sales manager of G-E Appliances' northwest region in 1927 and, in 1930, its Pacific Coast area.

After ten years in field sales, Cordiner was promoted to Manager of Heating Devices in the Appliance and Merchandise Division of General Electric. The Cordiners moved to Bridgeport, Connecticut, where the division was headquartered. There he became a protégé of Charles E. Wilson[b], Division Manager and Vice President. In 1935, Cordiner was promoted to Assistant Division Manager.

When Wilson became Executive Vice President of General Electric in 1938, Cordiner succeeded him as head of the Appliance and Merchandise Division. However, believing that he would remain in Wilson's shadow, Cordiner left GE in 1939 and accepted the

---

[a] *Walla Walla Union Bulletin,* April 18, 1968.
[b] Charles Edwin Edwin Wilson would later be dubbed "Electric Charlie" to distinguish him from Charles Erwin Wilson "Engine Charlie" of General Motors when both were active in U.S. government services during World War II.

presidency of the Magazine Repeating Razor Company, marketing Schick razor blades.

Wilson was President of General Electric from 1939 to 1942. He left General Electric to become vice-president of the War Production Board (WPB). Cordiner joined him there as Director General of War Production Scheduling.

Wilson returned to General Electric in 1945 and brought Cordiner along as his assistant. Cordiner was made a Vice President and, in 1949, elevated to the board of directors as Executive Vice President. This placed him in line to succeed Wilson.

General Electric was involved in 11 antitrust suits from 1911 through 1945. In 1946, as a response to these suits, GE formulated a corporate directive that stated it "is the policy of this company to conform to the antitrust laws." Directive Policy 20.5 was repeatedly revised until it eventually read (in part): "It is the policy of the company to comply strictly in all respects with the antitrust laws. There shall be no exception to this policy ... No employee shall enter into any understanding, agreement, plan, or scheme, express or implied, formal or informal, with any competitor, in regard to prices, terms or conditions of sale, production, distribution, territories, or customers." Every manager was periodically asked to indicate in writing that he was adhering to the policy. In this regard, managers were accountable directly to GE's headquarters, and any disciplinary action to enforce the policy would come from there; "In 1949, three General Electric employees, who were engaged in price-fixing acrobatics at the time, (were) quietly eased out by Cordiner..."[a]

When Wilson became director of the Office of Defense Mobilization in 1950, he was succeeded at General Electric by Philip Reed as Chairman of the Board and Chief Executive Officer. Cordiner

[a] *The Gentlemen Conspirators: The Story of the Price-Fixers in the Electrical Industry*, John G. Fuller.

became President and functioned as chief operating officer. In 1958, Reed would step down, and Cordiner would become Chairman of the Board and CEO.

Between 1950 and 1954 Cordiner devoted himself to reinventing the General Electric organization. He believed that the inflexibility of GE's centralized organization structure made it difficult to manage the business for maximum profit; GE had become too big to react quickly to changes in the diverse markets it served. Implementation of Cordiner's ideas began in early 1951. They were well established by 1953 when his *Professional Management in General Electric* detailed the new management concept in four booklets:

- *Book One: General Electric's growth*
- *Book Two: General Electric's Organization*
- *Book Three: The Work of a Professional Manager*
- *Book Four: The Work of a functional Individual Contributor.*

Cordiner saw General Electric as tightly tied to the phenomenal growth of electricity in the United States and world wide. He visualized a "benign circle of electric power."

> A turbine-generator installed in a power station makes possible the sale of more lamps, appliances, motors and other users of power. And as more people buy lamps, appliances and so on, they create the need for another turbine-generator and more transmission equipment. Thus each new use of electricity accelerates the turn of the circle – creating a bigger potential market for General Electric products, not only in end-use customer equipment, but in equipment to produce, transmit and distribute electric power.[a]

---

[a] *New Frontiers For Professional Managers*, New Corporate Dimensions, Ralph J. Cordiner.

Cordiner viewed General Electric as being or becoming the leading supplier of manufactured products to virtually all the markets in this 'circle of electric power' – managed by professional managers for maximum profit.

To achieve and maintain that position, he developed a radically different decentralized organization concept of around 100 'product departments' to develop, produce and market products to specific markets. Each product department was to function as an almost-autonomous business, under a General Manager responsible for maximizing profits over the long run; Cordiner emphasized that "The price of a product can be raised or lowered by the managers of the Department producing it."

Departments serving similar market areas (e.g., consumer, defense, federal government, industrial, utility, etc.) plus a number of sales and service departments were placed in 21 Divisions reporting to 7 Executive ("Group") Vice Presidents.

> Each division might be described as a family of businesses; for example, the Turbine Division consists of the Gas Turbine Department, the Large Steam Turbine-Generator Department, the Medium Steam Turbine, Generator and Gear Department, the Small Turbine Department, and the Foundry Department.[a]

Group Vice Presidents were members of the Executive Office at corporate headquarters. This line organization was supported by corporate-level staff operations such as legal, public relations, research, stockholder relations, treasury, etc., the heads of which were also members of the Executive Office. Staff operations were to advise and assist, but had no direct authority over line managers and their operations. "Thus each Executive Vice President serves as the

---

[a] *New Frontiers For Professional Managers*, Decentralization: A Managerial Philosophy, Ralph J. Cordiner.

President in a defined Operating area, without in any sense relieving the corporate President of the ultimate responsibility placed upon him by the Board of Directors ...[a]

Figure 10-1. Picture of Steam turbine generator from 1957 General Electric Annual Report.

> As of (1956), the Company's sales volume consists of approximately 35% consumer products, 25% user products for business and industry, 20% highly engineered defense, electronics, and atomic products, and 20% components and materials chiefly for other manufacturers. This diversity brings the Company into active competition with about 600 other principal companies ...
>
> General Electric has, in the United States, 138 plants in 107 cities in 28 states. In addition, the Company operates a number of atomic energy installations for the government and has sales or production facilities in may foreign countries.

---

[a]   Ibid.

In 1955, the Company's sales volume amounted to $3,095,000,000, and net earnings after taxes were $201,000,000. The Company's objective is to double its dollar sales volume by 1963 and improve its rate of earnings.[a]

In early 1959, the Tennessee Valley Authority's[b] frustration over years of identical bids from electrical manufacturers gained the attention of the press, then the Kefauver Antitrust Subcommittee of the Senate and the Antitrust Division of the Department of Justice. All began to dig. A federal grand jury in Philadelphia began to issue subpoenas to all major manufacturers in the electrical industry for their records back to 1956.[c] It became the biggest price-fixing antitrust investigation in U.S. history. The volume of records was so great that an additional four grand juries had to be impaneled to consider it all!

In an effort to determine what cards the government might be holding, General Electric sent its Trade Regulation Counsel, Gerard Swope, Jr., to look over its Pittsfield operations (turbine, transformer and switchgear divisions were headquartered there).

Mr. Swope, an amiable man, explained that his object was to reassure rather than worry the managers ... he privately reported, "the primary purpose of the meeting was not to interrogate the managers as to whether they had agreed or conspired with their competitors to fix prices; with all our admonitions and teachings during the years, and the positive company antitrust policy, I assumed there was no question on this score; rather the meeting was to explore with them the possibility of adopting a more dynamic pricing policy to get away from the consistent identity of prices which had

---

[a] *New Frontiers For Professional Managers,* New Corporate Dimensions, Ralph J. Cordiner.
[b] Tennessee Valley Authority (TVA) is the largest generator/supplier of electricity in the United States.
[c] The statute of limitations for violations of the Sherman Act is five years; violations in 1956 were as far back as indictments in 1961 could cover.

resulted in so many public criticisms … and which enhanced the exposure of the company to investigation and charges based on circumstantial evidence."

These words represent the precise degree of determined aloofness from the possibility of … knowledge by the topmost echelon of General Electric of what was going on in the marketplace.[a]

In mid-February 1960, the grand juries handed down the first of 20 true bills indicting 29 manufacturers and 45 of their officials (originally, 48; charges against 3 individuals were dropped for lack of sufficient evidence) of colluding to fix prices of electrical apparatus in violation of the *Sherman Antitrust Act*. General Electric was named as a co-conspirator in 19 of the true bills.

No trials were ever held. All defendants ultimately pleaded guilty or *nolo contendere*.[b] Top General Electric (and Westinghouse) executives denied any knowledge of the price-fixing activities.

Corporate fines ranged from $2,000 – $50,000 on any single count; General Electric was fined a total of $407,500 on 19 counts. Seven corporate executives, including two from GE, served 30-day jail sentences (27 days after time off for good behavior); 23 others, including eight from GE, got suspended jail sentences. All 45 individual defendants, 19 of them G-E personnel, were assessed fines ranging from $1,000 to $7,000.

But the matter didn't end there. The Kefauver hearings with public testimony went on for more than two years, during which time witnesses testified to the depth and breadth of the conspiracy.

---

[a] *The Great Price Conspiracy: The Story of the Antitrust Violations in the Electrical Industry*, Chapter II, John Herling.

[b] A '*nolo*' (no-contest) plea means the defendant neither accepts nor denies guilt, but is subject to the same punishment as with a "guilty" plea. This plea eliminates for both government and defendant the time and expenses of a trial and, for the defendant, it forecloses any trial evidence that might be used in a subsequent civil action.

Corporate representatives had been holding regular price meetings for many years, even back to 1946. They included informal and formal talks and agreements over prices and allocations of business for specific products and product categories. They included agreements as to which company was to be awarded each job put out for bid, with secret formulas to determine the prices that each company would bid to secure that end. Nothing was ever put in writing.

Witnesses before the Kefauver subcommittee confirmed, in effect, all the charges. The reams of testimony describing what went on included these snippets from General Electric employees:

William S. Ginn, Vice President and General Manager of, first, GE's Transformer Division and, later, the Turbine Division described meeting with competitors as far back as 1946 when he was a salesman for one of the transformer departments. One day, his sales manager invited Ginn along to a meeting with competitors to agree on prices for a specific bid. After the meeting, the sales manager directed Ginn to henceforth be the GE contact man for such meetings.

By October 1947, Ginn had become manager of power transformer sales. He still reported to the same sales manager, and kept him informed of all the price-fixing activities.

As a result of GE's 1950 organizational restructuring, Ginn began reporting to W.V. O'Brien, a vice president of apparatus sales who, in turn, reported to H.V. Erben, an Executive Vice President reporting directly to the president (Charles E. Wilson).

> According to Ginn, Erben ... told him that the market was getting "chaotic" – a favorite term which the industry uses when prices are getting down ... and suggested that Ginn had better go out and see what he could do about it ...
>
> In 1954, Ginn says that Cordiner called him to New York just before he took over as General Manager of the Transformer Division, and warned him to stay in line with

the antitrust laws. He also claims that this warning lasted just about as long as it took him to get back to Erben's office.

According to Ginn, Erben said, "Now, keep on doing the way you have been doing, but just be sensible about it and use your head on the subject."

In January of 1957, Ginn became Vice President and General Manager of the giant Turbine Division. Again, Cordiner … warned him about antitrust violation.[a]

Ginn signed Directive Policy 20.5 several times before and after these meetings. But he disregarded it just as "everybody else in the business seemed to be doing." Ginn explained this by saying that "after he had signed it, he was given other orders to the contrary by his superiors."[b]

George E. Burens, Vice President and General Manager of GE's Switchgear and Control Division, along with three others, implicated Arthur Vinson, Executive (Group) Vice President of Heavy Apparatus who reported directly to Ralph Cordiner. In discussions with investigators, all independently reported a particular meeting in the summer of 1958, which included Arthur Vinson, in which they had discussed meetings with competitors to "stabilize" prices. All four swore under oath, and passed related lie-detector tests, that Vinson there gave them the clear go-ahead to meet with competitors. Vinson declined to take a polygraph test. Charges against him were dropped because of insufficient corroborating evidence.

Another long-time General Electric employee provided the Kefauver Subcommittee intricate details of the price fixing. **Raymond W. Smith**, Vice President and General Manager of the Transformer Division, became a willing witness for the government, and during the Kefauver hearings, after what he viewed as unfair treatment by GE

---

[a] *The Gentlemen Conspirators: The Story of the Price-Fixers in the Electrical Industry*, John G. Fuller.

[b] Ibid.

Directive Policy 20.5 specified that employees who violated the policy were subject to disciplinary actions up to and including termination. But prior to 1958 no employee had ever been disciplined for violating the policy. After the grand juries began meeting, G-E. corporate officers, led by Cordiner, decided to institute a three-year 'statute of limitations' to 20.5; no employee would be disciplined if their policy violations had ceased more than three years before the violation came to light. The effect of this revision was to insulate top executive management who had handed off such activities to subordinates.

Ray Smith, who had joined General Electric in 1928, was not insulated. He testified before the Kefauver Committee that "during the entire period from 1940 through 1956 , it was common practice in (the switchgear and transformer) areas to discuss prices and other competitive matters with competitors ... I was also aware that similar practices were being followed ... in other areas of the company ... In other words, although the General Electric Policy 20.5 regarding antitrust practices had been issued in 1946, it had been consistently disregarded in major areas of the company with, at least, the tacit approval and agreement of managers and officers of the company at the time responsible for these areas." This included men who were by then executives in the Corporate offices. Smith testified for days about these activities and how he had kept his superiors, including Arthur Vinson, fully informed.

> With this background and understanding, Smith suffered an incredible shock when Cordiner, Paxton and Vinson lowered the boom on him and his subordinates. He was informed in November, 1959, that because of his actions in this area, his departmental managers and he were to be severely disciplined by the Company. This would include demotion, loss of title, substantial reduction in pay ... and transfer from

his home in Pittsfield. By this time, Smith was an angry, middle-aged corporate man.

> "Neither my people nor I acted in any way contrary to what was required of us in our jobs ... I felt that our activities had been carried on with the approval of my superiors ... the discipline proposed was most unfair to my people and me and that I could not ... participate in a program which seemed to me to be punishing some men by the retroactive application of new standards to activities previously carried on by them in the reasonable belief that they were in accord ... with the actual practices of this company ... Rather than consenting to become a part of such a plan, I resigned."[a]

Smith took a $10,000 job with a car rental agency, a far cry from the perks-laden $100,000 or so he had been getting from General Electric. And he testified for days before the Justice Department and, later, before the Kefauver Committee.

In addition to fines of $405,700 assessed in 1960, General Electric ultimately paid many millions of dollars in civil suits, and GE promised (with limitations) to never do it again.

> (AP) Washington July 27, 1962: General Electric Co. has agreed to pay a record $7.47 million to settle damage suits that followed conviction of the company in a price-fixing case ...
>
> In New York, Chairman Ralph J. Cordiner of GE termed the settlement reasonable and fair. "Now that these landmark cases are settled, GE hopes that in all other cases voluntary settlements can be negotiated to ensure equity to all parties involved and avoid years of costly contentious litigation," he said.
>
> If settlement can be achieved with all GE customers for these products on the basis used by the company in determining its offer to the government and TVA, the

---

[a]   *The Great Price Conspiracy: The Story of the Antitrust Violations in the Electrical Industry*, Chapter III, John Herling.

company's total price adjustment would be about $45 to $50 million over the next few years," Cordiner estimated.

General Electric and 19 of its officers and employees were punished for violations of antitrust laws that took place over a four-year period. No charges were brought for violations prior to 1956. General Electric paid millions to settle civil lawsuits.

Epilogue

Ralph J. Cordiner ordered demotions, reductions in pay and forfeitures of titles and perks for all 19 G-E personnel indicted and punished by the government but, as far as can be determined, not for others who participated in illegal activities prior to 1956.

General Electric stockholders addressed Cordiner and the G-E directors over the price-fixing, but the critics were few.

TIME, Friday May 05, 1961:
Management: Confidence in Cordiner
To the stockholders of General Electric, Chairman Ralph J. Cordiner clearly had some explaining to do about the conviction of 16 executives for price fixing. As the company's 69th annual meeting convened in Syracuse last week, Cordiner got right down to it, and with no apology in his voice. "It has been said by some," he said, "that I as chairman and chief executive officer, either knew of these violations and condoned them or that I was derelict in not knowing of them." Neither is true, said Cordiner. "We were diligent in the light of the facts as we then knew them."

When Cordiner finished his explaining, the inevitable sniping began …

Then James Carey, president of the International Union of Electrical Workers … cited the speech made two weeks ago by G.E. director Henry Ford II, in which he declared that business had better clean its house …

But ... the vast majority of the 2,700 shareholders at the meeting supported the company and Cordiner ...

After the meeting, the directors re-elected Cordiner to the chairmanship and also elected him president, a post he has filled since last February when Robert Paxton, one of the men currently in the price-fixing headlines, resigned, giving ill-health as the reason.

Cordiner never accepted any personal responsibility for the illegal activities of General Electric or its employees going back many years. But, while not admitting it ever had, the Company promised to never again commit the crimes for which it had plead guilty. (The promise was limited to just those specific crimes.)

AP Philadelphia September 26, 1962
General Electric Co. Tuesday promised the federal government it would never fix prices, rig bids, or restrict, suppress, limit or prevent competition in the sale of heavy equipment used in the generation and distribution of electric power in the United States,

The sweeping consent decree ... ended the criminal and civil antitrust actions brought against the nation's largest electrical manufacturer in 1960.

Cordiner was never held personally accountable for any of these crimes; he never paid any restitution or suffered any personal consequences. But did he know? Or tacitly condone? Or, in the past, even participate? We do not know. Cordiner repeatedly denied any knowledge of these illegal activities. He did know, however, of past violations of antitrust laws and Policy 20.5; "In 1949, three General Electric employees, who were engaged in price-fixing acrobatics at the time, (were) quietly eased out by Cordiner..."

Ralph J. Cordiner died on December 5, 1963.

Chapter 11:
Analysis and Discussion – Ralph J. Cordiner/ General Electric Company

Ralph J. Cordiner clearly knew that General Electric had engaged in price fixing and other antitrust activities in the past.

It may reasonably be inferred that he was aware of price-fixing of heavy electrical apparatus in the present, well before any charges were brought. How could he not know?

Customers had been grumbling for years. Cordiner knew the G-E operations more intimately than anyone else. Executive Vice Presidents reporting directly to him knew, and had been involved in the past. When he explicitly directed specific operational employees to adhere to 20.5, his Executive Vice Presidents immediately countermanded his orders; would they have done that if they had not thought Cordiner condoned the price fixing?

Judge J. Cullen Ganey, who presided over the judicial matters, thought that the corporate leaders, including Cordiner, condoned the illegal activities of their employees. He said:

> "This court has spent long hours in what it hopes is a fair appraisal of a most difficult task ... it is not at all unmindful that the real blame is to be laid at the doorstep of the corporate defendants and those who guide and direct their policy ... one would be most naive indeed to believe that these violations of the law, so long persisted in, affecting so large a segment of the industry and, finally, involving so many millions upon millions of dollars, were facts unknown to those responsible for the conduct of the corporation ..."[a]

---

[a]   *The Great Price Conspiracy: The Story of the Antitrust Violations in the Electrical Industry,* Chapter XIII, John Herling.

Even if Cordiner didn't know, he should have. The Board of Directors put him in charge. He was the boss. The operations and activities that produced profits (or losses) and produced returns for General Electric stockholders were his responsibility.

But Cordiner was a member of the Board of Directors. It did not sanction him in any way; he suffered no reductions in compensation or benefits. He remained Chairman of the Board. Only one member of the Board (Henry Ford II) spoke critically of the scandalous price-fixing activities.

Cordiner carefully avoided a personal paper trail – written and personal directives – concerning questionable General Electric activities. Thus, he was able to claim ignorance of nefarious activities and, in Policy 20.5, Cordiner built a mechanism that he and others in his executive offices used for plausible deniability.

Moreover, Cordiner was Chairman of the Board of Directors to which he nominally reported. Four of the six critical accountability conditions were absent in Ralph J. Cordiner's actions related to General Electric.

2. There was no personal superior-subordinate relationship; Cordiner did not report to anyone.

3. A one-to-one superior-subordinate relationship did not exist. Cordiner reported to a group – the Board of Directors – of which he was a member.

5. Other G-E officers were also members of the Board of Directors. Thus, Cordiner wielded substantial influence over some of those in the group to which he was nominally accountable.

6. Though the Board of Directors had authority to censure, restrain or otherwise significantly affect Cordiner, no one person had that authority; it would take a majority vote.

Conclusions

Ralph J. Cordiner created the General Electric organization concept and structure over which he presided. That philosophy placed responsibility for profitability, including pricing, in people far down the organization hierarchy. Profitability was the key performance criteria that determined department managers' evaluations, compensation and advancement. And earnings-per-share is, arguably, the dominating criteria used by boards of directors of most businesses in evaluating their CEOs.

Cordiner also strengthened and re-issued Policy 20.5 to, ostensibly, ensure that G-E people would not conspire with competitors to fix prices or otherwise violate antitrust law. He required that relevant G-E personnel certify they would abide by the policy. It is not known whether Cordiner, himself, ever signed such certification, but he certainly used it to assert plausible deniability.

Cordiner was never censured or held accountable in any meaningful way for the illegal price-fixing by General Electric and its employees. He might have been had he not been a member of the Board of Directors.

Questions to Consider

* Was Directive Policy 20.5 an effective mechanism for ensuring that General Electric personnel not conspire with competitors to fix prices or otherwise violate antitrust law? Why or why not?

- Suppose all members of the General Electric Board of Directors had been "outside" directors. Would that have improved accountability?
- Relevant laws generally shield corporate officials from liability for corporate actions, unless their knowing personal culpability can be proved. Should these laws be changed? In what ways?

Chapter 12:
Additional Reading – Ralph J. Cordiner/ General Electric Company

Fuller, John G. *The Gentlemen Conspirators: The Story Of The Price-Fixers In The Electrical Industry.* Grove Press, 1962.

 Herling, John. *The Great Price Conspiracy: The Story of the Antitrust Violations in the Electrical Industry*. Van Rees Press, 1962.

Walton, Frederick W. Jr and Cleveland, Clarence C. *Corporations On Trial: The Electric Cases*. Wadsworth Publishing Company, 1964

Also, search the internet for topics such as: General Electric, General Electric Company, Ralph J. Cordiner, Price-Fixing in the Electrical Industry, Electric Industry Price-Fixing, etc.

Case 4:

J. Edgar Hoover/Federal Bureau of Investigation

Chapter 13:
Executive Summary

John Edgar Hoover was born January 1, 1895, in Washington DC, 14 years before the forerunner of the FBI was established. He attended George Washington University where he got a Master of Law degree in 1917. During World War II he took a draft-exempt job with the Department of Justice in its War Emergency Division. He soon advanced to lead its Alien Enemy Bureau with authority to arrest and jail allegedly disloyal foreigners without trial.

After anarchists began bombing attacks on national leaders, the Bureau of Investigation, established in 1908, launched its General Intelligence Division, with Hoover at its head. One of his first assignments was to coordinate and carry out raids that resulted in thousands of arrests, often without warrants. These raids were much criticized for blatant civil rights abuses.

Hoover's career as an anti-Communist crusader was launched. He began keeping files, both official and personal, on virtually everyone investigated by his agents. And he used them.

At this time the U.S. Department of Justice had a reputation as a corrupt place for rewarding political hacks and others with high-paying jobs. Its Bureau of Investigation was no model of efficiency, and it, too, had gained a reputation for politicized investigations.

In 1924, President Calvin Coolidge named Harlan Fiske Stone as Attorney General. Stone appointed Hoover Acting Director of the Bureau of Investigation. Hoover agreed to take the job provided it be divorced from politics and not be a catch-all for political hacks. He insisted that appointments be based on merit, and the Bureau be responsible only to the the Attorney General. Stone added that Bureau activities must be limited to investigations of law violations, and incompetent or unreliable personnel be fired. Hoover was to nominate men of good character and ability. And improve the morale of the Bureau.

Hoover rebuilt the Bureau of Investigation from top to bottom. He improved morale among agents and others he retained. On December 10, 1924, Stone made the 29-year-old J. Edgar Hoover permanent Director of the Bureau of Investigation.

Hoover viewed the BI as his personal fiefdom, a law enforcement institution without peer, with himself the one person responsible for all its successes and glory. This mystique would blossom during the 1930s.

The *Federal Kidnapping* Act (Lindbergh Law), signed into law in 1932, gave the federal government jurisdiction in all cases that involved kidnapping. That changed in 1934 after the 'Union Station Massacre' in which gunmen killed two Kansas City police officers, one BI agent, the McAlester, Oklahoma police chief and outlaw Frank Nash.

The Union Station Massacre outraged the nation. J. Edgar Hoover vowed that "those who participated in this cold-blooded murder will be hunted down." All the perpetrators were eventually caught or killed. Later in 1934 Hoover and Attorney General Cummings lobbied Congress for a package of nine major crime bills that gave the federal government a comprehensive criminal code. Using its expanded jurisdiction, the Bureau organized special operations in 1934 to get John Dillinger, Baby Face Nelson and other notorious gangsters.

In July 1935, as the capstone of its newfound identity, the Bureau was renamed the Federal Bureau of Investigation. FBI agents had become, by this time, the only government employees known as "G-men."

During World War II the FBI was tasked with a growing counter-espionage portfolio requiring vast increases in staffing. A de facto direct reporting relationship between Hoover and President Roosevelt virtually eliminated Justice Department control over the FBI. More than that: Hoover provided Roosevelt with hundreds of reports on his political enemies, and Roosevelt protected Hoover and the FBI with unwavering public endorsement and support.

The *Communications Act of 1934* included a provision that "no person not being authorized by the sender shall intercept any communication and divulge or publish the existence, contents, substance, purpose, effect, or meaning of such intercepted communication to any person." Hoover got President Roosevelt to grant exception to the FBI in many, loosely-defined conditions; the FBI generally ignored the ban during World War II, and since.

FBI total employment rose from around 2,400 in 1940 to 13,317 by the end of the war; the number of special agents jumped to 5,702. These agents were mostly hired soon aster graduation from college and formally indoctrinated into the FBI culture.

The FBI, along with several other U.S. agencies, had engaged in foreign intelligence in many countries prior to World War II. Hoover wanted all foreign intelligence to be coordinated through the FBI, but Roosevelt made the OSS responsible for all foreign intelligence (except military intelligence) outside the western hemisphere; he made the FBI responsible for all foreign intelligence in North and South America.

When president Roosevelt died on April 12, 1945, Vice President Harry S Truman became president. Truman did not like J. Edgar Hoover. He cut short Hoover's attempt to establish a close personal connection; the day after Roosevelt's death he told Hoover to route matters that needed his immediate attention through his military aide.

Nevertheless, the FBI was soon carrying out secret investigations for the White House.

By 1951 responsibility for all foreign intelligence activities outside the United States had been assigned to other agencies. The FBI was assigned primary responsibility for counterintelligence within the United States – protecting the United States against foreign espionage and sabotage, especially by the Soviet Union.

The Republicans won the congressional elections of 1946. Hoover soon linked up with the House Un-American Activities Committee (HUAC). He agreed to provide it information from FBI files on scores of film and radio personalities. These became HUAC's bases for virtually all of its highly publicized investigations. A decades-long partnership was cemented between HUAC and the FBI.

In 1948, the FBI, for the first time, tried to oust a President. In the primaries it provided derogatory information on Harold Stassen to Thomas Dewey's campaign operatives. In the general election it provided Dewey's campaign with derogatory information on President Truman. Nevertheless, Truman won re-election.

In 1949, 28-year-old Judith Copland, a Justice Department employee, was arrested and charged with spying for the Soviet Union. Her trial began in April, and it looked like an open-and-shut case; evidence from FBI memorandums was overwhelming. But there was a second trial wherein Copland's attorney claimed there had to have been an illegal wiretap. Justice Department attorneys admitted as much and more.

Reacting to this revelation, Hoover established procedures to shield such files from public and even legal scrutiny by breaking comprehensive files into many separate files with innocuous titles and storing them in a separate area under continuous surveillance.

At this time J. Edgar Hoover believed Communism was the greatest threat to America. He became friends with Wisconsin's

Senator Joseph McCarthy and helped him with his anti-Communist rantings. Hoover saw that McCarthy got useful information from FBI files and strategic advice from FBI personnel. He suppressed information that might be damaging to McCarthy.

Hoover supported Dwight D. Eisenhower in his 1952 presidential campaign, both with information smearing Adlai E. Stevenson, Eisenhower's opponent, and by leaking that information to the press (most of the press covered it up). Hoover also suppressed potentially damaging information on Richard M. Nixon, Eisenhower's running mate. Eisenhower won the election. Hoover reportedly viewed the next eight years as "the best and happiest years he ever had."

In 1954, Hoover obtained formal authority for microphone surveillance; prior to that time FBI bugs were widely employed but generally illegal. The FBI would make extensive use of that authority.

In 1956 the FBI launched secret "counter-intelligence-programs" (COINTELPROs) directed against persons and organizations deemed by Hoover to be subversive. In addition to the Communist Party of the U.S.A. and related entities, COINTELPROs eventually targeted a long list of civil rights and Black activist organizations and their leaders, some white-supremacy organizations such as the Ku Klux Klan, new-left, anti-war groups and the American Indian Movement. The FBI used surveillance, wiretaps, bugs and illegal entries, mail openings, planted 'evidence', public smearing and direct violence in these programs. Bogus documents and evidence were leaked to the press. Agents infiltrated targeted organizations and often incited them to violence and murder. COINTELPROs were ended in 1971 after a burglary of an FBI office revealed their existence.

Hoover favored Richard M. Nixon in the 1960 presidential election, and provided the campaign useful information from FBI files. Covering his bases, he also supplied assistance to John F. Kennedy.

After Kennedy was elected President, one of his first acts was to appoint his brother Robert as Attorney General. Hoover was not pleased. Quiet dislike and antagonism between Hoover and his new boss went back to the Eisenhower years when Robert was special counsel to a senate committee investigating organized crime. Hoover's public position at the time was that there is no such thing as a "mafia" or "organized crime."

However, Hoover was enlightened in November 1957, by a police raid in Apalachin, New York during a meeting of crime figures from around the country and Canada. Days later, Hoover inaugurated the FBI's Top Hoodlum Program, which led to a bug being planted in a Chicago tailor shop used as a meeting place by Chicago mob bosses. That bug soon made the FBI the most knowledgeable agency on organized crime in America. However illegal it was, the bug stayed in place for more than five years.

In May of 1962, Hoover reprised a ploy used eight years earlier by directing a memo to Byron White, Deputy Attorney General, pointing out that then Attorney General Brownell had approved the use of such bugs. The claim was disingenuous in its omitting many conditions Brownell had applied to his limited authorization. Neither Robert nor John Kennedy ever expressed objection, so Hoover got extended authority for expanded illegal bugging.

President Kennedy was assassinated on November 22, 1963, and Vice President Lyndon B. Johnson (LBJ) became President.

J. Edgar Hoover and President Johnson liked each other, and they routinely helped each other. LBJ used the FBI to provide information on his political enemies, and give him advance warning when something unfavorable was about to be publicized. LBJ never missed an opportunity to praise Hoover publicly, and he enjoyed the more salacious parts of wiretaps forwarded to his attention.

LBJ appointed Nicholas Katzenbach to succeed Robert Kennedy, who resigned as Attorney General in September 1964. Katzenbach disliked Hoover, but was instructed to get along. Nevertheless, Katzenbach believed that Hoover's unlimited license to bug was not legal, and he acted to reign it in. In March 1965, Katzenbach directed that Hoover's bugs be initiated only with the same authorization as wiretaps. He also ordered that wiretaps be reevaluated every six months and continued only with specific new authorization by the Attorney General. Growing and more frequent conflicts between the two led to Katzenbach's resigning as Attorney General effective on November 28, 1966.

During the last half of the 1960s, J. Edgar Hoover came under increasing attack from Justice and others within the administration, from Congressmen and Senators, and from the press. Hoover believed that offense is the best defense, so he generally took that approach when confronted with threats. And though he was careful to maintain deniability, his modus operandi was essentially blackmail.

The first step was to maintain or create a suitable weapon – information that, if made public, would be extremely damaging to his antagonist. The second step was to make sure the adversary knew of the information in Hoover's possession, and understood that it would be made public if the adversary didn't accede to Hoover's demands. The final step, if needed, was to make the information public to 'destroy' the antagonist. And while Hoover used FBI personnel and resources for these activities, he was careful that no paper trail or other evidence would lead directly back to him.

Inside the 'beltway' J. Edgar Hoover was widely acknowledged to be virtually untouchable. Many in Washington eagerly anticipated his mandatory retirement at age 70 on January 1, 1965. However, by executive order President Lyndon B. Johnson exempted him "from compulsory retirement for an indefinite period of time."

In March of 1968 Lyndon Johnson announced that he would not run for reelection. A scramble erupted among presidential hopefuls. Virtually all of them were viewed by Hoover as unfriendly or outright enemies to himself and the FBI. So he helped the Republican ticket.

Richard M. Nixon won handily. After the election President Johnson told Nixon that J. Edgar Hoover had been critically helpful to him during his presidency. He advised Nixon to retain Hoover as Director of the FBI, which Nixon already intended to do. At Hoover's request, Nixon announced that decision in mid-December.

Nixon promised Hoover direct access to him at any time, but he immediately nullified that promise by instructing his chief of staff that nobody was to have such access. Of course, Hoover soon knew that Nixon had broken his promise.

Very much aware of his predecessors' use of the FBI for personal political purposes, Nixon was soon asking Hoover for the same. By that time Hoover was growing fearful that leaked information about illegal FBI activities would reflect badly on the FBI and embarrass him, personally. So he began insisting that all requests for specific FBI activities be in writing, and he increasingly withheld authorization for such. But Hoover was losing some of his former total control; FBI agents, Special Agents in Charge (SACs) and others were increasingly using illegal techniques without specific authorization.

Throughout most of his career, public criticism of and attacks on J. Edgar Hoover were rare. But such became almost routine in 1971, growing to a crescendo. By the end of the year calls for his resignation or replacement were raised by congressmen and in editorials, from White House personnel, and even among FBI agents. It seemed possible that Hoover would be called before Congress or even eventually charged with crimes.

But he wasn't. Instead, J. Edgar Hoover died at his home on May 2, 1972. An autopsy was not performed: official cause of death was listed as "hypertensive cardiovascular disease."

The Attorney General immediately sealed Hoover's office as part of an intense search for Hoover's secret files. But the files had never been there. They had always been in the office of Hoover's personal secretary, who removed the files and destroyed them.

Chapter 14:
Father of The FBI Culture

Figure 14-1. J. Edgar Hoover FBI Building in Washington D.C.

John Edgar Hoover was born January 1, 1895, in Washington DC, 14 years before the forerunner of the FBI was established. He was the youngest of four children born to Dickerson and Annie Marie Hoover. His father was a career bureaucrat with the U.S. Coast and Geodetic Survey.

> Annie Hoover dominated the household ... she held to old-fashioned virtues and made sure her offspring did likewise. Her influence on her youngest – whom she called Edgar and the rest of the family referred to as J.E. – was particularly strong ... Edgar never married. He lived with his mother in the (family) house until she died. He was then 43 years old ...

> Although he taught Sunday school, and for a time served
> as assistant superintendent of the church's junior department,
> Hoover fatefully chose another career. But he retained a
> lifelong conviction that he had been ordained to distinguish
> right from wrong.[a]

Hoover would live in the same house in Washington DC his entire life. He attended Central High School, where he sang in the school choir, participated in ROTC, and competed on the debate team. He was valedictorian of his high-school class. He got his first job as a messenger in the Library of Congress, just a half mile from his house; he was 18 years old.

The University of Virginia offered Hoover a scholarship, but he enrolled close to home in night school at George Washington University where he joined Kappa Alpha fraternity. He got a Bachelor of Laws degree in 1916 and a master's in 1917.

America entered World War I on April 6, 1917. Hoover qualified, through ROTC, for a military commission upon graduation, but he did not enlist. He took a draft-exempt job with the Department of Justice in its War Emergency Division, and he soon advanced to lead its Alien Enemy Bureau with authority to arrest and jail allegedly disloyal foreigners without trial. Hoover would join the Bureau of Investigation (BI), forerunner of the FBI, in 1919.

The Bureau of Investigation had been established in 1908. Soon after President Theodore Roosevelt named Charles Bonaparte Attorney General in 1906, Bonaparte became frustrated over his lack of investigators; he had to use operatives from the Secret Service who reported to the Chief of the Secret Service. Bonaparte had little control over his own investigations.

Then, in 1908, Congress banned the loan of Secret Service operatives to any other federal department. So, in late June of that

---

[a]   *J. Edgar Hoover: The Man and the Secrets*, Chapter 4, Curt Gentry.

year, Bonaparte formed a special agent force of 34 investigators. On July 26, 1908 he ordered Department of Justice attorneys to refer most investigative matters for handling by one of these 34 agents. That date is recognized as the official birth of the FBI. In 1909 Bonaparte's successor, Attorney General George W. Wickersham, dubbed these agents "the Bureau of Investigation."

BI agents initially investigated mostly antitrust, land fraud, banking fraud, naturalization and copyright violations, and peonage (forced labor). The BI also handled a few national security issues, including treason and anarchist activity. In 1910 it took the investigative lead in the newly passed *White Slave Traffic Act* (Mann Act), an attempt to halt interstate prostitution and human trafficking. By 1915, the number of Bureau personnel had grown to around 360 special agents and support personnel.

The BI soon became involved in national security work through offices on the Mexican border that investigated smuggling and neutrality violations. When the United States entered World War I, Congress passed the *Espionage Act* and later the *Sabotage Act*. Enforcement was assigned to the BI, thus putting it in the counter-spy business. The BI was also tasked with rounding up deserters and policing millions of "enemy aliens" – Germans in America who were not American citizens.

The Bolsheviks took over Russia in 1917 and were soon talking world-wide revolution. Americans became concerned over such talk as they faced widespread labor and economic unrest. Hoover was made special assistant to the attorney general in charge of counter-radical activities.

After anarchists began bombing attacks on national leaders, the BI launched its General Intelligence Division (GID). BI Chief Flynn named J. Edgar Hoover to head this division, and ordered investigation of all anarchists, Bolsheviks and related agitators. One of Hoover's first assignments was to coordinate and carry out the Palmer Raids,[a] which resulted in around 3,000 arrests, often without warrants, and more than 500 deportations. These raids were much criticized for blatant civil rights abuses.

> Although stating the investigations should be directed particularly to aliens, for the purpose of developing deportation cases, Flynn added, "you will also make full investigation of similar activities of citizens of the United States with a view to securing evidence which may be of use in prosecutions under the present existing state or federal laws or under legislation of that nature which may hereinafter be enacted ..."
>
> In short, in addition to investigating aliens for possible deportation, for which neither the Justice Department nor the Bureau of Investigation had statute authority, America citizens should also be investigated, anticipating that perhaps someday Congress might pass laws covering their beliefs and associations, too.[b]

Hoover's career as an anti-Communist crusader was launched, and he began cultivating political connections. One of these arranged for Hoover to be commissioned a reserve Army officer and be assigned to Military Intelligence. (Hoover would advance to Lieutenant Colonel by the time he resigned his commission in 1942 after 20 years service.) By this time Hoover had already become the most knowledgeable person in government as regarded American radicalism. He began keeping files, both official and personal, on virtually everyone investigated by his agents. And he used them.

"For more than three decades, Hoover had access to, and traded information with, a privately financed intelligence network of civilian,

---

[a]   The Palmer Raids targeted suspected socialists and Eastern European immigrants, especially anarchists and communists.

[b]   *J. Edgar Hoover: The Man and the Secrets*, Chapter 6, Curt Gentry.

military and police spies – without the knowledge or consent of any of his superiors, be they attorneys general or presidents."[a]

In 1921, in addition to continuing as chief of the GID, Hoover was made Assistant to BI Chief William J. Burns, "the colorful and cheerfully crooked founder of the famous Burns Detective Agency."[b]

That same year, Hoover's father died. Hoover became his mother's only support and lived with her until her death in 1938. Annie and "J.E." frequently clashed over household matters; Hoover was described as a tyrant by nearby relatives.

Hoover's almost puritanical concern over image led to a permanent change in personal identification around this time.

> Hoover's good name meant a great deal to him. While applying for a charge account in a downtown store, he was denied credit. Asking the reason, he learned there was another John Edgar Hoover in Washington, who had been running up bills and bouncing checks all over town. From then on he signed all his memos "J. Edgar Hoover."[c]

At this time the U.S. Department of Justice had a poor reputation. Inside Washington it was often referred to as the Department of Easy Virtue, a corrupt place for rewarding political hacks and others with high-paying jobs that carried no specific responsibilities. Its Bureau of Investigation was no model of efficiency, and it, too, had gained a reputation for politicized investigations.

In 1923 BI Chief Burns sent three agents to Montana to dig up dirt on Montana's U.S. Senator Burton Wheeler. Wheeler and Thomas Walsh, Montana's other Senator, were spearheading the Senate investigation of the Teapot Dome Scandal.

---

[a] *J. Edgar Hoover: The Man and the Secrets*, Chapter 9, Curt Gentry.
[b] *The Director: My Years Assisting J. Edgar Hoover*, Chapter 1, Paul Letersky.
[c] Ibid.

Back in Washington, Bureau agents placed the two senators, their families and their friends under surveillance ...

They also ... tapped telephones, intercepted mail, broke into offices and homes, and copied correspondence and papers, looking for anything which might be used for blackmail.[a]

In 1924, soon after the news of these secret activities broke, President Calvin Coolidge fired Attorney General Daugherty and named Harlan Fiske Stone as his successor. Stone fired Burns and appointed Hoover Acting Director of the Bureau of Investigation.

Hoover agreed to take the job under these conditions: "The Bureau must be divorced from politics and not be a catch-all for political hacks. Appointments must be based on merit ... and the Bureau will be responsible only to the the Attorney General."

Stone also had conditions: Bureau activities to be limited to investigations of law violations; eliminate unneeded personnel; fire incompetent or unreliable personnel; eliminate most "dollar-a-year" men;[b] for new appointments, nominate men of good character and ability; improve the morale of the Bureau.[c]

Hoover rebuilt the Bureau of Investigation from top to bottom. And he did it quickly. By doing so he improved morale among agents and others he retained and, of course, he made enemies.

Attorney General Stone was impressed. On December 10, 1924, he made the 29-year-old J. Edgar Hoover permanent Director of the Bureau of Investigation. Hoover would hold that position until his death in 1972.

Hoover demanded much of his employees, and himself. His entire life was the Bureau. He typically worked six days a week and part of Sunday, and he took work home virtually every night. He also had a

---

[a] Ibid.

[b] Dollar-A-Year men had independent means and took government jobs at virtually no salary in order to get around budget limitations.

[c] *J. Edgar Hoover: The Man and the Secrets*, Chapter 10, Curt Gentry.

direct telephone line installed to his home; if anything happened warranting his attention he was to be notified immediately. That phone rang a lot.

Hoover had already won a decision that was critical to his avoiding accountability. He had begun keeping files on individuals who were not under investigation, files that could be used to 'influence' such individuals who might otherwise damage Hoover's position. In an August 1924 meeting among American Civil Liberties Union founder Roger Baldwin, Attorney General Stone and Hoover, Baldwin referred to such files on himself and the ACLU and asked that they be destroyed. Backed by Hoover's research into the statutes, Stone "told Baldwin that without an act of Congress he lacked the authority to destroy the master index and personal files compiled by his predecessors."[a] Kept in the office of Hoover's personal secretary until Hoover died, those "secret" personal files were never included in the master index. Decades would pass before anyone would again challenge them.

Soon after Franklin D. Roosevelt was inaugurated president in 1933 he signed an executive order extending civil service to most departments of the federal government. This would mean that Hoover could no longer arbitrarily fire BI employees he found wanting. The power to do so had been critical in his rebuilding the Bureau, and was essential to his maintaining personal control. Hoover determined to retain it.

> Hoover ... fought to keep the Bureau of Investigation exempt. Promotions should be based on ability, Hoover argued, not seniority. Also, he stated quite bluntly that he would resign before being forced to accept Communists and other undesirables. Although the battle raged over many years, hearings, and court decisions, Hoover eventually succeeded in keeping the Bureau civil service exempt.

---

[a] Ibid.

This meant that he could hire or fire, promote or demote, anyone he chose, without having to justify his actions or have them subject to review. Few others, no matter how high in government, had such unlimited power. J. Edgar Hoover would retain *and use* it until the day he died.[a]

Hoover viewed the BI as his personal fiefdom, a law enforcement institution without peer, with himself the one person responsible for all its successes ... and glory. This mystique would blossom during the 1930s. The glorifying began, however, in 1925 when the Bureau took over the investigation of the Osage Murders.

In May 1921, the badly decomposed body of Anna Brown – an Osage Native American – was found in a remote ravine in northern Oklahoma. The undertaker later discovered a bullet hole in the back of her head.

... just two months later, Anna's mother ... suspiciously died. Two years later, her cousin ... was shot to death. Then, in March 1923, Anna's sister and brother-in-law were killed when their home was bombed. One by one, at least two dozen people in the area inexplicably turned up dead ...

a slew of private detectives and other investigators turned up nothing ... The Osage Tribal Council turned to the federal government, and Bureau agents were detailed to the case.

Early on, all fingers pointed at William Hale ... (who) had bribed, intimidated, lied, and stolen his way to wealth and power. He grew even greedier in the late 1800s when oil was discovered on the Osage Indian Reservation. Almost overnight, the Osage became incredibly wealthy, earning royalties from oil sales through their federally mandated "head rights."

Hale's connection to Anna Brown's family was clear. His weak-willed nephew ... was married to Anna's sister. If Anna, her mother, and two sisters died – in that order – all of the "head rights" would pass to the nephew ... and Hale could take control ...

---

[a] *J. Edgar Hoover: The Man and the Secrets*, Chapter 12, Curt Gentry.

> Solving the case was another matter. The locals weren't talking … So four of our agents got creative. They went undercover as an insurance salesman, cattle buyer, oil prospector, and herbal doctor to turn up evidence. Over time, they gained the trust of the Osage and built a case. Finally … The agents were able to prove that Hale ordered the murders … In January 1929, Hale was convicted and sent to the slammer. His henchmen … also got time.[a]

The FBI's published synopsis of that case is revealing for what it doesn't say. Not there or anywhere in its official history can be found the name of former Texas Ranger Tom White, or of the others White independently recruited; they didn't fit Hoover's specifications for BI agents. FBI records don't note that only Ernest Burkhart, John Ramsey and William Hale actually went to prison; they were given life sentences, but Ramsey and Hale were released after serving 10 and 20 years, respectively. FBI records also don't mention that the case was closed without trying anyone for most of the 24 murders investigated, or even investigating scores or hundreds of other Osage murders over a period of several years before and after the three trials were concluded.

The 1920s and 1930s were years of lawlessness in the United States, fueled first by prohibition and later by the great depression. "Gangster era" activities of the 1920s generally occurred in and around big cities, the major markets for illicit booze. The BI lacked jurisdiction and was relegated to a supporting role in most prohibition cases; Treasury agents got most of the publicity. That was to change.

On March 1, 1932, the infant son of Charles and Anne Lindbergh[b] was abducted from his crib in the Lindbergh's New Jersey home.

---

[a] https://www.fbi.gov/history/famous-cases/murder-and-mayhem-in-the-osage-hills. Also, David Grann's *Killers of the Flower Moon* is a riveting history of the Osage Murders and the men who solved them.
[b] Charles Lindbergh was a U.S. Air Mail pilot who flew the first airplane non-stop cross the Atlantic Ocean in 1927.

Ransom was paid. On May 12, the child's corpse was discovered by the side of a road. Many state and federal agencies were on the case but, in October 1933, President Roosevelt ordered that all investigations be coordinated by the Bureau of Investigations. Bruno Hauptmann was found by New Jersey authorities in 1934 (the BI was involved and claimed credit). The case led to the *Federal Kidnapping* Act (Lindbergh Law), signed into law in 1932, which gave the federal government jurisdiction in all cases that involved kidnapping.

The few years from 1934 through 1936 form the "Public Enemy Era" popularized by depression-era outlaw-heroes. Most of these men (and at least a couple women) were born in the Midwest and committed their crimes in rural areas and small towns. They kidnapped businessmen, robbed banks (in at least one case carrying off all the bank's credit and loan records), and killed many lawmen in the process. But except in cases of kidnapping, the federal government had little jurisdiction in the early 1930s. That changed in 1933-1934.

In 1932, outlaw Frank Nash escaped from the United States Penitentiary in Leavenworth, Kansas. On June 16, 1933, two federal agents and the McAlester, Oklahoma police chief captured Nash in Hot Springs, Arkansas. They then drove with Nash to Fort Smith and boarded a train for Kansas City. They had contacted the Special Agent in Charge (SAC) of the BI's Kansas City office to meet them at Kansas City's Union Station upon arrival the next morning. When they walked out of Union Station into the parking lot they were ambushed by several gunmen. During the 30 seconds or so of gunfire two Kansas City cops, one BI agent, the Oklahoma police chief and Frank Nash were killed. The incident was front-page news all across America.

> Kansas City, June 17, 1933. (AP) – Underworld machine gunners shot and killed four officers and their prisoner, Frank Nash, Oklahoma train robber, in front of the Union Station here today ...

> Officials differed on whether the attack was an attempt to free Nash ... or whether the main purpose of the gangsters was to kill the outlaw ...
>
> The killers, believed to number four, fled in an automobile with their sub machine guns barking after surprising the officers and deliberately shooting them down ...
>
> R.E. Vetterli, Chief of the United States bureau of investigation for Kansas and western Missouri, exchanged shots with the slayers and escaped injury as did Frank Smith, a Department of Justice investigator.

The 'Union Station Massacre' outraged the nation. J. Edgar Hoover vowed that "those who participated in this cold-blooded murder will be hunted down." All the perpetrators were eventually caught or killed.

Hoover and Attorney General Cummings used the Union Station Massacre and the Midwestern crime wave to lobby Congress for a package of nine major crime bills in 1934.

> The new laws were ... "one of the most important, if least recognized, New Deal reforms." They gave the federal government ... a comprehensive criminal code ...
>
> The Bureau was no longer limited to investigating white-slave cases, interstate auto theft, and federal bankruptcy violations. Under the new laws, the robbery of a national bank or a member bank of the Federal Reserve System was made a violation of federal law, as were the transportation of stolen property, the transmission of threats, racketeering in interstate commerce, and the flight of a felon or witness across state lines to avoid prosecution or giving testimony. The Lindbergh Law was amended to add the death penalty and to create a presumption of interstate transportation of the victim ... And special agents of the Bureau of Investigation were given the right to make arrests, execute warrants, and carry firearms, while the killing or assaulting of a government agent was made a federal offense.

Quietly and without publicity … Hoover used part of his appropriation to go shopping for "hired guns" – former lawmen with practical police experience …

Few had attended college … and none fit Hoover's prescribed image of a special agent. Most wore cowboy boots and Stetsons and carried their own guns … and all were inclined to react out of instinct and experience rather than according to the manual. But Hoover was wise enough to realize he needed them, for a time. Although they attained legendary status within the Bureau, and figured prominently in some of its most famous early cases, Hoover made sure their exploits and backgrounds went unpublicized.[a]

The Bureau had arrested "machine gun" Kelly in 1933. And using its expanded authority, the Bureau took down a succession of what it listed as 'Public Enemies': Bonny & Clyde, John Dillinger, "Pretty Boy" Floyd and Baby-Face Nelson were killed in 1934; "Doc" Barker was arrested and "Ma" Barker and her son Fred were killed in 1935; Alvin Karpis, the brains of the Barker gang, was captured in 1936.

The Bureau organized a special operation in 1934 to get John Dillinger. Melvin Purvis, the Bureau's Chicago SAC, reported a tip that Dillinger and his gang had been spotted at a resort in Wisconsin. Hoover immediately ordered agents from Chicago and Saint Paul to race to the area. After nightfall they surrounded the resort and shot three innocent men they mistakenly thought were part of the Dillinger gang. The gang escaped. Newspapers had a heyday.

About a month later Purvis got a tip that Dillinger was in Chicago and would be attending a movie at the Biograph Theater. This time they got him; shot him dead in an alley beside the theater. Hoover had been informed; he waited by his telephone until the movie was over and Dillinger was confirmed dead. Hoover then made the announcement to the press.

---

[a]   *J. Edgar Hoover: The Man and the Secrets*, Chapter 13, Curt Gentry.

Dillinger's straw hat and his Colt .38 were put in a display case near Hoover's office where they remained until after Hoover's death 38 years later.

A short time later Purvis led the agents who trapped Baby Face Nelson in Indiana and shot him to death. To Hoover's chagrin, newspapers made Purvis a national hero. That put him on Hoover's enemies list. Hoover rewrote Bureau reports of the cases to minimize or remove Purvis' name from the records.

In July 1935, as the capstone of its newfound identity, the Bureau was renamed the Federal Bureau of Investigation. FBI agents had become, by this time, the only government employees known as "G-men."[a]

> The killing wasn't all a one-way street; five Bureau agents died in gun battles with the gangsters. But every killing and every arrest made headlines for Hoover and his G-men … Hollywood started making gratuitously violent films that glorified the G-men. The most famous was *G-Men* (1935) … but there were dozens of others, with titles such as *Let 'Em Have It*, *Show Them No Mercy!*, and *Public Hero Number 1*. There were G-men radio shows, G-men books, G-men comic strips. And there were countless newspaper and magazine stories about … J. Edgar Hoover.
>
> … almost overnight Hoover became much more than just a government official. On paper he may have been a $6,000-a-year (about $100,000 today) midlevel bureaucrat, but in real life he was a celebrity. Soon his distinctive bulldog face could be spotted at star-rich venues such as the Stork Club in New York … he was photographed with stars from little Shirley Temple to the sultry Dorothy Lamour. The Gangster Era made J. Edgar Hoover – and the FBI.[b]

---

[a]   Before 1934, "G-Man" was underworld slang for any government agent.
[b]   *The Director; My Years Assisting J. Edgar Hoover*, Chapter 1, Paul Letersky.

Around this time Hoover made a powerful enemy in Congress, In 1933 he had refused to appoint constituents of Tennessee Senator Kenneth McKellar special agents. McKellar, chairman of the subcommittee in charge of appropriations for the Department of Justice, complained to the Attorney General. Hoover then fired three special agents from Tennessee. McKellar didn't forget.

In early 1936 Hoover was testifying before the Senate subcommittee to ask for an appropriation of $5 million to implement the new crime laws, about twice his estimate when testifying in support of them. Senator McKellar grilled and berated Hoover mercilessly about FBI advertising and public relations expenditures, killing of people with guns, involvement with Hollywood film producers, and several other issues. When the bill came before the full Senate it appeared that the requested appropriation was destined to be cut, but Democrat Senators were persuaded that cutting FBI funds was bad election-year politics. The FBI got its appropriation and McKellar went on Hoover's enemies list (ultimately warranting several FBI dossiers including one in Hoover's Official/Confidential files[a]). McKellar never again opposed Hoover.

About this time Hoover made a powerful ally, President Franklin Delano Roosevelt. Roosevelt and Hoover 'understood' each other, particularly, how to serve each other's interests while enhancing their own. Roosevelt made no notes of many of their meetings, which was often/usually the case when he was discussing sensitive or illegal matters in private. But Hoover did.

> On August 24, 1936, Franklin Delano Roosevelt summoned J. Edgar Hoover to the White House for a private meeting ...
> According to Hoover, the president ... wanted to discuss "subversive activities in the United States, particularly Fascism and Communism" ...

[a]   *J. Edgar Hoover: The Man and the Secrets*, Chapter 15, Curt Gentry.

Hoover told the president that the FBI lacked authority to conduct such an investigation. Roosevelt asked if he had any suggestions. Hoover just happened to know of a loophole. "I told him that the appropriation of the Federal Bureau of Investigation contains a provision that it might investigate any matters referred to it by the Department of State and that if the State Department should ask for us to conduct such an investigation we could do so under our present authority."[a]

Of course, the FBI received that request from Secretary of State Cordell Hull. The ensuing investigation would make extensive use of wiretaps and other techniques that Hoover had opposed since the 1920s. His opposition to wiretaps and such evaporated just before and during World War II.

During the war hundreds of FBI wiretaps and bugs were planted in the embassies and consulates of governments considered friendly to the Axis powers and were deployed against people suspected of espionage and sabotage. The practice continued during the 1950s and into the mid-1960s, when the Bureau routinely wiretapped and/or bugged Communist Party members, organized crime figures, Klansmen, neo-Nazis, and suspected "subversives" ... all under the category of "internal security" and all without a warrant.

And the Bureau was good at it. Every major field office had a team of "soundmen," agents who were specially trained in wiretapping and the use of ... listening devices. They were also trained in lockpicking, safecracking, defeating alarm systems, and other skills necessary for black bag jobs.[b]

World War II provided countless opportunities for Hoover to enhance his autonomy and expand the FBI's scope. The FBI was tasked with a

---

[a]   Ibid.
[b]   *The Director; My Years Assisting J. Edgar Hoover*, Chapter 4, Paul Letersky.

growing counter-espionage portfolio requiring vast increases in staffing. And a defacto direct reporting relationship between Hoover and President Roosevelt virtually eliminated Justice Department control over the FBI. More than that: Hoover provided Roosevelt with hundreds of reports on his political enemies, and Roosevelt protected Hoover and the FBI with unwavering public endorsement and support.

As was done before his time, Hoover used the FBI to discredit and smear his opponents. Case in point: In 1940 Congressman Martin Dies of Texas wanted his House Committee on Unamerican Activities to be given law enforcement status co-equal with the FBI.

> Hoover ... launched an intensive behind-the-scenes campaign to discredit Dies. FBI agents were sent to spy on the committee; its findings were ridiculed, sometimes even before they saw print. Lists were made of Dies's anti-administration remarks; rumors ... were reported as fact. Derogatory information on Dies was leaked to the president, the attorney general, other congressmen, and favored press contacts.[a]

Dies went to Roosevelt, and Roosevelt suggested he meet with the Attorney General "to see if something could be done to eliminate such misunderstandings." A deal was struck: The committee agreed to clear any information it uncovered with the Department of Justice so as to not interfere with any secret FBI investigation. The machinery thus created would thereafter be used to smear thousands of Americans.

The *Communications Act of 1934* included a provision that "no person not being authorized by the sender shall intercept any communication and divulge or publish the existence, contents, substance, purpose, effect, or meaning of such intercepted communication to any person."[b] Hoover got president Roosevelt to

---

[a] *J. Edgar Hoover: The Man and the Secrets*, Chapter 19, Curt Gentry.
[b] The 1934 Act has been amended and superseded many times, but that proscription is still law. Ref 47 U.S. Code § 605.

grant exception to the FBI in many, loosely-defined conditions; the FBI generally ignored the ban during World War II, and since.

> Buggings, wiretapping, break-ins mail opening, and telegraph and cable monitoring – these were only some of the illegal acts which, adopted under the guise of "wartime necessity" and found to be highly useful shortcuts, became standard, albeit secret, investigative tools of Hoover's FBI.[a]

The FBI more than quintupled in size during the war years; total employment rose from around 2,400 in 1940 to 13,317 by the end of the war; the number of special agents jumped to 5,702.[b] None of these agents were "hired guns" as had been the case during much of the 1930s; they were mostly hired soon after graduation from college and formally indoctrinated into the FBI culture.

> According to (William) Sullivan, he and his fellow World War II classmates developed a particular mindset that would stay with them throughout their Bureau careers: "We never freed ourselves from the psychology that we were … just like a soldier in the battlefield. When he shot an enemy he did not ask himself: is this legal or unlawful, is it ethical? It was what he was supposed to do as a soldier.
> "We did what we were expected to do. It became part of our thinking, part of our personality."
> Having been taught to disregard "the niceties of law," they continued to disregard them through the Cold War, the Korean War, the Vietnam War and in the COINTELPROs – the FBI's own war on Dissent (1956-1971).[c]

The FBI, along with several other U.S. agencies, had engaged in foreign intelligence in many countries prior to World War II. Hoover wanted all foreign intelligence to be coordinated through the FBI, but

---

[a]   *J. Edgar Hoover: The Man and the Secrets*, Chapter 20, Curt Gentry.
[b]   Ibid.
[c]   Ibid.

on that issue he was opposed by virtually all the other intelligence chiefs in the government. His arch competitor William Donovan, head of the recently established Office of Strategic Services (OSS), also wanted dominion over all intelligence services.

In 1942 Hoover and Donovan each submitted a plan to Roosevelt. The Donovan plan might have been accepted, but Hoover leaked news of it to a newspaper, and the resulting story caused Roosevelt to kill the plans of both Donovan and Hoover. He made the OSS responsible for all foreign intelligence (except military intelligence) outside the western hemisphere, and he made the FBI responsible for all foreign intelligence in North and South America.

President Roosevelt died on April 12, 1945. Within days Hoover's called Lou Nichols in Crime Records and ordered him to bring in all the files on Harry S Truman.[a]

Truman did not like J. Edgar Hoover. He cut short Hoover's attempt to establish a close personal connection; the day after Roosevelt's death he told Hoover to route matters that needed his immediate attention through his military aide, Brigadier General Harry Vaughan. So ...

> That same day Hoover sent Vaughan a memo beginning, "I thought you and the President might be interested to know ..." He then went on to report some political intelligence.
>
> Vaughan responded by asking for more: "future communications along that line would be of considerable interest"
>
> Hoover also sent confidential reports to other presidential aides ...
>
> Within thirty days after Truman became president, the FBI was carrying out secret investigations for the White House ...

---

[a] *J. Edgar Hoover: The Man and the Secrets*, Chapter 21, Curt Gentry.

Truman was compromised before he knew it.[b]

In May 1945, Truman appointed Tom Clark Attorney General. Clark "showed no inclination to actually supervise the FBI."[b] He had an assistant screen all memos from Hoover and, unknowingly, he even broadened Hoover's powers.

> On July 7. 1946. the attorney general wrote the president asking him to renew Roosevelt's 1940 warrantless wiretapping authorization. Although Clark's letter quoted from that authorization, it omitted a key sentence: "You are requested furthermore to limit these investigations ... to a minimum and ... insofar as possible to aliens."
>
> The elimination of that single sentence ... gave Hoover nearly unlimited authority to place as many wiretaps as he wanted, on whomever he chose.
>
> Truman approved ... unaware that anything had been omitted or that the ... letter had actually been drafted by J. Edgar Hoover.[c]

Germany surrendered on May 7, 1945, followed by Japan on August 14. In September, President Truman abolished the OSS, eliminating Hoover's most serious competitor. But Hoover didn't gain much.

By 1951 responsibility for all foreign intelligence activities outside the United States had been assigned to other (not FBI) agencies such as Army (MID) and Navy (ONI) intelligence and the new Central Intelligence Agency (CIA). The FBI was assigned primary responsibility for counterintelligence within the United States – protecting the United States against foreign espionage and sabotage,[d] especially by the Soviet Union.

---

[b]   *J. Edgar Hoover: The Man and the Secrets*, Chapter 22, Curt Gentry.
[b]   Ibid.
[c]   Ibid.
[d]   See https://www.fbi.gov/investigate/counterintelligence

The Republicans won the congressional elections of 1946. Hoover soon linked up with the House Un-American Activities Committee (HUAC). He agreed to provide it information from its files on scores of film and radio personalities that Hoover felt had communist connections. These became HUAC's bases for virtually all its highly publicized investigations of alleged communist infiltration of the movie and broadcast industries. A decades-long partnership was cemented between HUAC and the FBI.[a]

In 1948, the FBI, for the first time, tried to oust a President. In the primaries it provided derogatory information on Harold Stassen to Thomas Dewey's campaign operatives. Arguably, the FBI information helped Dewey win the primary. In the general election the FBI provided Dewey's campaign with derogatory information on President Truman. Nevertheless, Truman won re-election.[b]

In 1949, 28-year-old Judith Copland, a Justice Department employee, was arrested and charged with spying for the Soviet Union. Her trial began in April, and it looked like an open-and-shut case; evidence from FBI memorandums was overwhelming. But J. Edgar Hoover later called the trial "one of the biggest disasters in the history of the (FBI),"[c] because it aired many of the Bureau's illegal activities and contents of secret files.

When arrested, Copland had in her possession 28 FBI documents including "data slips" that summarized specific FBI reports, along with her note reading, "I have not been able ... to get the top secret FBI report ... on Soviet and Communist activities in the U.S. ..."

When the data slips were introduced into evidence at the trial, defense counsel requested that the documents on which they were based also be entered into evidence. When informed, Hoover urged

---

[a] *J. Edgar Hoover: The Man and the Secrets*, Chapter 23, Curt Gentry.
[b] Ibid.
[c] *J. Edgar Hoover: The Man and the Secrets*, Chapter 24, Curt Gentry.

Attorney General Clark to seek a mistrial or contempt citation rather than produce the documents, which could "because of the contents of these particular files, embarrass the FBI ... since the files contained unverified gossip and accusations ..."[a]

The judge ordered the government to produce the reports.

> It was a historic moment: the first time anyone outside the government had seen copies of raw FBI files ... One report identified the Hollywood actors Frederic March, Helen Hayes, John Garfield ... and Paul Muni as "Reds." There were slanderous remarks about ... prominent persons ... as well as gossip about relative unknowns ... And there was much more, little having to do with real government secrets, much having to do with politics ..."[b]

There was more to come. A second trial for Copland and a United Nations employee who was her lover/Soviet contact was scheduled for December. After examining the mass of evidence, Copland's court-appointed attorney concluded that there had to have been an illegal wiretap.

Justice Department attorneys admitted as much and more: contrary to sworn testimony of the FBI agent, there had been taps throughout the first trial on Copland's home and office phones and on her parents' phone. Among other items, these taps picked up conversations between Copland and her attorney. The Judge learned that "some thirty agents had participated in the eavesdropping," and that the taps were ordered removed "just prior to the start of the (first) trial, a month earlier."[c]

Reacting to this revelation, Hoover established procedures to shield such files from public and even legal scrutiny by breaking

a   Ibid.
b   Ibid.
c   Ibid.

comprehensive files into many separate files with innocuous titles and storing them in a separate area under continuous surveillance.

In 1963 during a retraining class of some 50 senior FBI agents, instructor Cartha DeLoach was asked what the Bureau did with all "this memorandum stuff we put in about things we see." DeLoach responded,

> "You fellows have been in the Bureau for more than ten years so I guess I can talk to you off the record. The other night we picked up a situation where this senator was seen drunk, in a hit-and-run accident, and some good-looking broad was with him. By noon the next day the good senator was aware that we had the information and we never had any trouble with him on appropriations since."[a]

After World War II, J. Edgar Hoover came to believe that Communism was the greatest threat to America. He became friends with Wisconsin's Senator Joseph McCarthy and helped him with his anti-Communist rantings. Hoover saw that McCarthy got useful information from FBI files and strategic advice from FBI personnel. He suppressed information that might be damaging to McCarthy.[b]

Hoover materially supported Dwight D. Eisenhower in his 1952 presidential campaign, both with information smearing Adlai E. Stevenson, Eisenhower's opponent, and by leaking that information to the press (most of which the press covered up). Hoover also suppressed potentially damaging information on Richard M. Nixon, Eisenhower's running mate.[c] Eisenhower won the election. Hoover reportedly viewed the next eight years as "the best and happiest years he ever had."[d]

---

[a] Ibid.
[b] Ibid.
[c] *J. Edgar Hoover: The Man and the Secrets,* Chapter 26, Curt Gentry.
[d] Ibid.

In 1954 Hoover obtained formal authority for microphone surveillance; prior to that time FBI bugs were widely employed but generally illegal. The Supreme Court had, that year, declared that local police bugging of a suspected gambler's bedroom was illegal. Hoover asked Attorney General Brownell how that decision should affect the FBI, and accompanied his question with a draft response. On May 20, 1954, Brownell responded:

> it is clear that in some instances the use of microphone surveillance is the only possible way of uncovering activities of espionage agents ... and subversive persons ... The FBI has an intelligence function in connection with internal security matters ... considerations of internal security and the national safety are paramount and, therefore, may compel the unrestricted use of this technique in the national interest.[a]

Hoover could henceforth bug anyone he chose, by whatever means he deemed necessary. The FBI would make extensive use of that authority.

In 1956 the FBI launched secret "counter-intelligence-programs" (COINTELPROs) directed against persons and organizations deemed by Hoover to be subversive. Initially, such included the Communist Party of the U.S.A. and related entities. COINTELPROs soon targeted what became a long list of civil rights and Black activist organizations and their leaders. Some white-supremacy organizations such as the Ku Klux Klan became subjects of COINTELPROs and, near the end of their operational life, COINTELPROs were deployed against new-left, anti-war groups and the American Indian Movement.

> There was a rash of campus bombing and arsons – sixty-one of them in the 1968-69 academic year alone – as well as violent takeovers of college buildings ... Coupled with

---

[a]   Ibid.

increasingly violent anti-war protests in the streets, the campus and civil unrest convinced J. Edgar Hoover, among others, that ... something had to be done ... in mid-1968 Hoover approved a plan to combat ... anti-war violence and civil disobedience.

The plan was COINTELPRO – New Left ... The Bureau would "expose, disrupt, misdirect, discredit and otherwise neutralize" the violent New Left groups that opposed the war and the US government, as well as the people who supported those groups. Students, professors, anti-war clergymen – all were potential targets.[a]

The FBI used surveillance, wiretaps, bugs and illegal entries, mail openings, planted 'evidence', public smearing and direct violence in these programs. Bogus documents and evidence were leaked to the press. Agents infiltrated targeted organizations and often incited them to violence and murder. All COINTELPROs were secret, and much or most of what they did was illegal.

During these years Hoover extended his influence to congressional committees by supplying them information from FBI files, and FBI personnel as full-time consultants. Former Agents were also appointed to influential positions in the state department and other government agencies. And, of course, there were 'the files'. Inside the 'beltway' J. Edgar Hoover was widely acknowledged to be virtually untouchable. Many in Washington eagerly anticipated his mandatory retirement at age 70 on January 1, 1965. However, by executive order President Lyndon B. Johnson would exempt him "from compulsory retirement for an indefinite period of time."

Hoover favored Richard M. Nixon in the 1960 presidential election, and provided the campaign useful information from FBI files. Covering his bases, he also supplied more than just token assistance to John F. Kennedy. His services to both campaigns included not

[a] *The Director: My Years Assisting J. Edgar Hoover,* Chapter 5, Paul Letersky.

releasing or leaking damaging information, which both candidates knew was in his personal files. During the campaign both candidates promised to retain Hoover as Director of the FBI.

After Kennedy was elected President, one of his first acts was to appoint his brother Robert as Attorney General. Hoover was not pleased; quiet dislike and antagonism between Hoover and his new boss went back to the Eisenhower years when Robert was special counsel to a senate committee investigating organized crime. Hoover's public position at the time was that there is no such thing as a "mafia" or "organized crime."

However, Hoover was enlightened in November 1957, by a police raid on a private estate in Apalachin, New York during a meeting of a hundred, or so, crime figures from around the country and Canada. Days later, Hoover inaugurated the FBI's Top Hoodlum Program, which led to a bug being planted in a Chicago tailor shop used as a meeting place by Chicago mob bosses. That bug soon made the FBI the most knowledgeable agency on organized crime in America. However illegal it was, the bug stayed in place for more than five years.

In May of 1962, Hoover reprised his ploy of eight years earlier by directing a memo to Byron White, Deputy Attorney General, pointing out that then Attorney General Brownell had approved the use of such bugs. The claim was disingenuous in its omitting many conditions Brownell had applied to his limited authorization. Neither Robert nor John Kennedy ever expressed objection, so Hoover got extended authority for expanded illegal bugging.

By 1963 the feud between Hoover and Robert Kennedy had heated up.

> The schism between the FBI director and the attorney general, which had grown most noticeably during 1963, was ... due to the fact "that Bobby mentioned to too many people

> ... 'Look, just wait,' and we all got the message that they were going to retire him after Jack got re-elected and Hoover hit seventy. And it got back to him. Hoover had too many spies and too many bugs not to have heard the talk.[a]

But President Kennedy was assassinated before he could be reelected, and Vice President Lyndon B. Johnson (LBJ) became President on November 22, 1963. As noted, on May 18, 1964, executive order 11154 exempted J. Edgar Hoover "from compulsory retirement for an indefinite period of time."

The relationship between J. Edgar Hoover and President Johnson could be characterized as symbiotic. They had known each other and socialized for years; Johnson and his family moved into a house near Hoover's in 1945.

> On occasional Sunday mornings, like a favorite uncle, Hoover would be invited over for breakfast with the family. The two Johnson girls, Lynda Bird and Lucy Baines, considered the country's number one G-man a protector. When their pet dog ran off somewhere in the well-tended shrubbery of the neighborhood, the congressman would ring the director's doorbell. "Edgar, little Beagle Johnson's gone again. Let's go find him." Or the girls would race over by themselves, certain that their avuncular friend would interrupt one of his cowboy TV shows and help them out.[b]

Hoover and Johnson liked each other, and they also both respected and feared each other. LBJ was very aware of Hoover's secret files on him, and he was also privy to information on Hoover and the FBI gathered by other government agencies.[c] And, of course, Johnson could retire Hoover at any time.

---

[a]   *J. Edgar Hoover: The Man and the Secrets*, Chapter 29, Curt Gentry.
[b]   *J. Edgar Hoover: The Man and the Secrets*, Chapter 30, Curt Gentry.
[c]   Ibid.

They routinely helped each other. LBJ used the FBI to provide information on his political enemies, and give him advance warning when something unfavorable was about to be publicized. LBJ never missed an opportunity to praise Hoover publicly, and he enjoyed the more salacious parts of actual wiretaps forwarded to his attention.

> Grave and statesmanlike for an Oval Office interview with newspaper reporters, (LBJ) paused thoughtfully when asked to name the "greatest living American.
> "J. Edgar Hoover." he finally replied. Without Hoover, this country would have gone Communist 30 years ago."
> In fact, President Johnson ... was never squeamish about the FBI director's output.
> "Who went with who, and who was doing what to who" ... came directly from Hoover to LBJ ...
> "He sometimes found gossip about other men's weaknesses a delicious hiatus from work," said Johnson's aide Bill Moyers, hinting that this interest may have inspired "constitutional violations" in pursuit of more of the same ...
> But LBJ recognized the two-edged nature of this type of weapon. At his request, tapes and memoranda documenting some of his own questionable activities – sexual and financial – were lifted from the raw files of the FBI and sent over to the White House. They have not been seen since.
> Even so, it was clear to Moyers that the president "personally feared J. Edgar Hoover."[a]

Robert Kennedy resigned as Attorney General in September 1964. LBJ appointed Nicholas Katzenbach to succeed Kennedy, initially as acting AG; five months later the 'acting' was dropped. Katzenbach disliked Hoover, but was instructed to get along with Hoover and the Bureau.[b]

Katzenbach believed that Hoover's unlimited license to bug was not legal, and he acted to reign it in. In March 1965, Katzenbach

---

[a] Ibid.
[b] Ibid.

directed that Hoover's bugs be initiated only with the same authorization as wiretaps. He also ordered that wiretaps be reevaluated every six months and continued only with specific new authorization by the Attorney General.

> These moves threatened a delicate balance that Katzenbach understood very well: "In effect, (Hoover) was uniquely successful in having it both ways. He was protected from public criticism by having a theoretical superior who took responsibility for his work, and was protected from his superior by his public reputation."
>
> Affable as he was bright, the attorney general tried to encourage personal meetings with Hoover ... He met with an icy chill. Hoover increasingly avoided contact with Justice officials, and with his own personnel as well ...
>
> Katzenbach knew that the FBI was leaking potentially embarrassing stories about him to the press ... During the 1975 Church committee hearings the astounded Katzenbach was shown three documents bearing his initials. Avoiding the term "forgery" he testified that he did not remember reading the documents and certainly would have. Each reported on an unauthorized bug on Martin Luther King, Jr. The FBI laboratory declared Katzenbach had indeed initialed the memorandums.[a]

Growing and more frequent conflicts between the two led to Katzenbach's resigning as Attorney General effective on November 28, 1966.

J. Edgar Hoover came under increasing attack during the last half of the 1960s, from Justice and others within the administration, from Congressmen and Senators, and from the press. Hoover believed that offense is the best defense, so he generally took that approach when confronted with what he viewed as significant threats. And though he

---

[a]   *J. Edgar Hoover: The Man and the Secrets*, Chapter 31, Curt Gentry.

was careful to maintain deniability, his modus was essentially blackmail.

The first step was to maintain or create a suitable weapon – information that, if made public, would be extremely damaging to his antagonist. Often that weapon was already in his secret files – evidence of criminal acts, political missteps, immoral behavior or peccadilloes that had been reported by FBI agents over the years. If file information was insufficient for his purposes, Hoover would see that it was generated – through false reports, planted evidence, induced testimony, etc.

The second step was to make sure the adversary knew of the information in Hoover's possession, and understood that it would be made public if the adversary didn't accede to Hoover's demands – usually to cease hostile hearings, retract statements, support budget requests, etc.

The final step, if needed, was to make the damaging information public in ascending stages – to the antagonist's family, political supporters, supervisors, the press, etc. until the antagonist was 'destroyed'.

And while Hoover used FBI personnel and resources for these activities, he was careful that no paper trail or other discreet evidence would lead directly back to him.

Published books and articles report on many such instances, but two recounted by Curt Gentry[a] serve to illustrate.

In 1965 **Senator Edward Long** of Missouri, who chaired the Subcommittee on Administrative Practice and Procedure, began looking into surveillance activities of government agencies. Concerned that Long's Subcommittee would uncover the FBI's unauthorized mail intercept programs, Hoover got President Johnson to have Attorney General Katzenbach coordinate the responses for all intelligence

---

[a]   Ibid.

agencies. Pressure was also brought on the chairman of the Senate Judiciary Committee to rein in Long. For a while it seemed to have worked.

But the press wouldn't drop the story, so Hoover increased the pressure. Long had been picked out in the FBI's coverage of organized crime; he had accepted campaign support money from the mob-dominated Teamsters Union. It was in Hoover's files, and he made sure Long knew it. After much back-and-forth, that, too, seemed to have worked.

But no. In the spring of 1967 Long's subcommittee readied proposed legislation to ban wiretapping and bugging except in national-security cases determined by strict guidelines. So the FBI leaked its file material to *Life* magazine. A May article posited that Long's committee was working to get a reversal of Teamsters president James Hoffa's earlier conviction for jury tampering.

A Senate committee exonerated Senator Long, but his career was over. His subcommittee's bill was set aside, and he was defeated in the primary when he ran for reelection.

In 1966 **Representative Cornelius Gallagher** of New Jersey, a member of the House Committee on Government Operations, became concerned about government abuse of surveillance capabilities. His Subcommittee on Invasion of Privacy was about to address potential threats by means of computer technology. Reportedly, Hoover was "sick and tired" of being criticized for illegal surveillance and wanted Gallagher's subcommittee to relieve him of the public criticism, presumably by calling off the hearings; Gallagher was contacted many times, but the hearings went forward.

Material from FBI files was leaked to *Life* magazine, which prepared a story for its August 9, 1968 issue. The story reported that a wiretap on organized crime had revealed information about a member of Congress. It alleged that Gallagher had suspiciously close ties with the head of Cosa Nostra's operations in Gallagher's hometown.

> Tagged "the tool and collaborator" of (the Cosa Nostra), Gallagher was quickly dropped from consideration for being raised in the hierarchy of House leadership. But Hoover was not satisfied. "(He wanted) him to resign from Congress."
>
> If he did not, the FBI was prepared to leak the story, which it was already spreading casually around town, that ... a minor mob figure, had died of a heart attack while making love to the congressman's wife.[a]

Gallagher threatened to further attack Hoover publicly, and demanded that the FBI announce that the supposed wiretap transcripts were false, which it did. But the rumors remained and, as with Long, Gallagher's career was over.

In March of 1968 Lyndon Johnson announced that he would not run for reelection. A scramble erupted among presidential hopefuls, and virtually all of them were viewed by Hoover as unfriendly or outright enemies to himself and the FBI. So he helped the Republican ticket, covertly in case the Democrat should win.

Richard M. Nixon won handily. After the election President Johnson told Nixon that J. Edgar Hoover had been critically helpful to him during his presidency. He advised Nixon to retain Hoover as Director of the FBI, which Nixon already intended to do. At Hoover's request, Nixon announced that decision in mid-December to preempt a *True* magazine "expose" of Hoover in its January 1969 issue.

> Of all the eight presidents he had served under while FBI director, Hoover knew this one best. His files on Nixon dated back to 1939 ... He knew his strengths and weaknesses. He knew of more crises than Nixon himself cared to remember.

---

[a] Ibid.

He was aware of financial and personal relationships that
had never surfaced during any of Nixon's campaigns.[a]

Nixon promised Hoover direct access to him at any time, but he immediately nullified that promise by instructing his chief of staff H.R. Haldeman that nobody was to have such access. John Ehrlichman, White House Counsel, then functioned as liaison with J. Edgar Hoover and the FBI. Of course, Hoover soon knew that Nixon had broken his promise.

Very much aware of his predecessors' use of the FBI for personal political purposes, Nixon was soon asking Hoover for the same. But by that time Hoover was growing more fearful that leaked information about illegal FBI activities would reflect badly on the FBI and embarrass him, personally. So he began insisting that all requests for specific FBI investigations and activities be in writing and signed by the President or Attorney General, and he increasingly withheld authorization for such. But Hoover was losing some of his former total control; FBI agents, SACs and others were increasingly using illegal techniques without specific authorization.

On Friday, June 5, 1970 … President Nixon summoned J. Edgar Hoover and CIA Director Richard Helms to the Oval Office, along with the chiefs of the National Security Agency and the Defense Intelligence Agency … the President lectured Hoover and the others that "revolutionary terrorism" now represented the single greatest threat against American society. He demanded that the four agencies assemble a concerted, overarching intelligence plan to defeat its spread.

At the FBI, Hoover's no. 2 man, Bill Sullivan, already had such a plan well in hand. The following Monday, June 8, he convened the first of five meetings to tear down the walls between the FBI, the CIA, and their brethren, lift all restrictions on domestic intelligence gathering, and clear the way for all four agencies to institute every dirty trick in the

[a] *J. Edgar Hoover: The Man and the Secrets*, Chapter 32, Curt Gentry.

FBI's old playbook: illegal break-ins, unilateral wiretapping, the opening of mail, even inserting information into undergraduate classrooms. They called it the Huston Plan, after Tom Charles Huston ... the Nixon aide who championed it alongside Sullivan ... on July 14, the president said he approved. There was just one problem: J. Edgar Hoover was dead set against the Huston Plan.

The old man had grown exceedingly cautious in his last years, fearful his legacy would be tarnished if the rampant illegalities he had ordered over the years burst into view ... his main objection was the question of blame if this ever became public. Nixon had given only verbal approval. Hoover, who had no idea that Sullivan had already cleared FBI offices to engage in almost all these illegal tactics, had no doubt he and the FBI would take the fall.[a]

Hoover had cut off all liaison with the CIA in March. Now he ordered liaison be ended with the National Security Agency, the Defense Intelligence Agency, the Secret Service, the Internal Revenue Service, and Army, Navy and Air Force Intelligence.

Hoover had triumphed, taking on and beating the president, his representative, and all three of the other intelligence chiefs. But at a tremendous cost. Now even the president agreed that Hoover would probably have to be replaced.[b]

A COINTELPRO against the Black Panthers, which had begun in late 1968, continued with its illegal activities unabated during the first three years of Nixon's presidency. However, in March 1971, an activist group burglarized the FBI's Media, Pennsylvania field office gave the press information it found there, including the existence of COINTELPROs. The FBI officially terminated this last COINTELPRO a month later. (The FBI did not, however, forever

[a] *Days of Rage*, Chapter 06, Bryan Burrough.
[b] *J. Edgar Hoover: The Man and the Secrets*, Chapter 33, Curt Gentry.

eschew the illegal and unethical techniques it had perfected, many of which have surfaced from time-to-time up to the present day.)

Throughout most of his career, public criticism of and attacks on J. Edgar Hoover were rare. But such became almost routine in 1971, growing to a crescendo. By the end of the year calls for his resignation or replacement were raised by congressmen and in editorials, from White House personnel, and even among FBI agents. It seemed possible that Hoover would be called before Congress or even eventually charged with crimes.

But he wasn't. Instead, J. Edgar Hoover died at his home. On May 2, 1972, his lifeless body was found by his bed. An autopsy was not performed. Official cause of death was listed as "hypertensive cardiovascular disease."

The Attorney General immediately sealed Hoover's office as part of an intense search for Hoover's secret files, but the files had never been there. They had always been in the office of Helen Gandy, Hoover's personal secretary. She removed and destroyed the files.

Epilogue

President Nixon named L. Patrick Gray III to be acting Director of the FBI. Gray resigned less than a year later after failing to get Senate confirmation as Director.

Just a month after Hoover's death, a burglary was discovered at Democratic campaign headquarters in the Watergate Hotel. The FBI investigated, ultimately identifying the perpetrators as members of the White House staff. Newspaper reporters also investigated, aided by a stream of FBI leaks from a source known at the time as "Deep Throat." Many years later Mark Felt, Gray's Deputy Director of the FBI, revealed himself as Deep Throat.

Many FBI Special Agents (SAs) weren't sure about what illegal tactics they could continue using in their investigations. And some were becoming discouraged by their lack of success in capturing members of the Weather Underground, a radical group known for its bombings.

> Questions about wiretaps and black bag jobs lingered all that summer in the chaos that pervaded FBI headquarters after Hoover's death. A new director, L. Patrick Gray, was named, but for months no one seemed to have a clear sense of how aggressively he wanted to pursue the Weather Underground … Finally, at a meeting of supervisors on August 29, Ed Miller pointedly asked Gray whether black bag jobs would still be allowed. According to Miller, Gray said they would. At the subsequent meeting, Miller recalled, "Gray stood up and he did tell them. He said he had decided to approve surreptitious entries, 'but I want you to make damn sure that none of these are done without prior bureau authorization." Afterword Miller telephoned one of his aides, Robert Shackleford to say break-ins would be resumed. "That's good," Shackleford said, "because they're going on anyway."
> Later that fall … President Nixon issued a secret presidential directive calling for an all-out counterterrorism campaign. In Gray's mind, at least, this included actions against the Weather Underground. He told his No. 2 man, Mark Felt, that he wanted the Weathermen "hunted to exhaustion." Newly emboldened, (the FBI) renewed its illegal activities with a vengeance, initiating black bag jobs against the friends and families of twenty-six Weather fugitives. It was all very secret and all, very clearly now, illegal.[a]

Grand jury investigations into illegal practices resulted in indictments of Gray, Felt and Miller in April 1978. These three were

---

[a] *Days of Rage*, Chapter 06, Bryan Burrough.

the only FBI or Justice Department personnel who would ever be tried for these practices.

> On September 15, 1980... W. Mark Felt and Edward S. Miller were finally brought to trial in a Washington federal court ... Their onetime boss, L. Patrick Gray, the man who had succeeded J. Edgar Hoover, was processed separately; the charges against him would later be dismissed altogether.
>
> The proceedings ... were thick with the air of anticlimax ... But there was no denying that, however dangerous the Weather Underground had been, the two FBI men had approved illegal activities in their efforts to apprehend its leadership. They were swiftly convicted. The men faced up to ten years in prison. Two months later the judge handed down their sentences: a $5,000 fine for Felt, $3,500 for Miller. Neither would serve jail time ... America yawned.[a]

Clarence Kelley became Director of the FBI on July 9, 1973. He had been an FBI Special Agent for more than 20 years until he retired in 1961 to become Police Chief of Kansas City, Missouri. He served as FBI Director until replaced in 1978 by William H. Webster. None of the six Directors since Kelley have had prior FBI experience.

In 1975 the Senate established a *Select Committee to Study Governmental Operations with Respect to Intelligence Activities* chaired by Idaho Senator Frank Church. It uncovered questionable and illegal activities of the CIA, NSA, FBI and IRS. Ensuing legislation included Public Law 94-503 (October 15, 1976) limiting the FBI Director to a single term of no longer than 10 years. In 1978 Congress enacted the *Foreign Intelligence Surveillance Act* (FISA) that established a Court to approve or (theoretically) deny applications for electronic surveillance, physical search, and other investigative actions for foreign intelligence purposes.

On February 19, 2004, CBS News reported:

---

[a] *Days of Rage*, Chapter 22, Bryan Burrough.

An internal FBI report kept under wraps for three years details dozens of cases of agents fired for egregious misconduct and crimes, including drug trafficking, attempted murder, theft, misuse of informants and consorting with prostitutes.

The report ... found that about one in 1,000 agents was dismissed for serious misconduct or criminal offenses ... from 1986 to 1999. The average was between eight and nine per year.

The report did not indicate that any of the offending agents was ever prosecuted.

Chapter 15:
Analysis and Discussion – J. Edgar Hoover/FBI

J. Edgar Hoover "retained a lifelong conviction that he had been ordained to distinguish right from wrong." Early in his career that motivated him to reform the Bureau of Investigation by ridding it of things that were not 'right', especially political influence and incompetent, unreliable and unneeded personnel. Hoover rebuilt the Bureau from top to bottom, improving its morale and effectiveness.

Hoover believed that he and the Bureau were one and the same, to be steadily strengthened and protected against all detractors, both inside and outside the government. In this he was aided by most of the Presidents he served under.

> Franklin Delano Roosevelt … did the most to expand the Bureau's – and Hoover's – authority and power. Roosevelt pushed the series of congressional "anti-crime bills" in the mid 1930s that greatly expanded the Bureau's … role beyond crime fighting and into domestic intelligence and internal security. Roosevelt … ordered Hoover to investigate political groups on the left and the right – Communists, Fascists, America First members who opposed US involvement in the war in Europe, and other political opponents of the president – and FDR secretly gave Hoover the authority to use wiretaps in "national security " cases. When Hoover took office in 1933 the Bureau had fewer than four hundred special agents in the ranks; by … 1945 , that number had grown … to forty-five hundred agents.[a]

In the mid-1920s Hoover began keeping "secret" files on persons he thought might become a threat or tool, including those to whom he

---

[a]   *The Director; My Years Assisting J. Edgar Hoover*, Chapter 4, Paul Letersky.

was or might become accountable. And he used those files to quash criticism, interference with Bureau activities and meaningful supervision.

By the early 1950s J. Edgar Hoover had established his political invulnerability to attempts to curb his or the FBI's power, whether from competitors such as Bill Donovan, congressional enemies, attorneys general, or even presidents.

From early on, Hoover avoided leaving paper trails that might lead back to him; he preferred that such trails lead back to his nominal superiors. Sometimes they did, especially during his early years with the Bureau. And Hoover often contrived to lay such paper trails. He became a master at subtle suggestions to Presidents and Attorneys General, and at burying authority within documents he drafted for his nominal superiors.

Hoover was often frustrated by legal limitations that made the FBI's tasks more difficult. He tried to work around them but couldn't always able do so. During World War II he got used to using whatever worked, in the interests of "national security." Using that sort of rationale his FBI developed and perfected a long list of illegal and unethical activities – wiretaps, bugs, break-ins, mail openings, planted evidence, false documents, leaks, rumor-mongering, etc.

> Hoover wasn't acting on his own. Since before World War II, every president he's served under – those revered by the left and those revered by the right – knew what Hoover and the Bureau were doing in domestic security and surveillance ... most didn't want to know the details – but they knew the general outlines. Every one of those presidents could have made Hoover stop what he was doing or fired him outright.[a]

---

[a]   Ibid.

Hoover's first-line weapons were his "secret" files, which caused almost everyone to conclude that "FBI Director J. Edgar Hoover was "too big to handle" ..."[a]

Four of the six critical accountability conditions were absent in J. Edgar Hoover's actions related to the FBI.

2. The superior-subordinate relationship was often impersonal. As Director of the FBI Hoover officially reported to a distanced Attorney General. And Hoover also reported to a President who did not require specific accountability

3. There wasn't a single one-to-one superior – subordinate relationship. Hoover 'reported' to the Attorney General, the President and to various committees of Congress and their chairmen.

5. Through his files, Hoover wielded usually subtle, always enormous influence with nominal superiors and others who could affect him or his FBI.

6. Attorneys General and Presidents had the power to censure, restrain or fire Hoover, but no one had the political courage or inclination to do so.

Conclusions

J. Edgar Hoover built the FBI over which he presided. Early on he set out to glorify the FBI and himself, and insulate both from criticism or censure. His successes led to growing arrogance and disrespect for differing opinions. He willfully averted accountability.

---

[a] *J. Edgar Hoover: The Man and the Secrets*, Chapter 25, Curt Gentry.

Hoover engendered a culture of 'ends justify the means' arrogance among many in the FBI, and an acceptance of using the FBI for purposes outside its legal scope of operations. Arguably, some or much of that culture remains to the present day.

Hoover was never censured or held accountable in any meaningful way for the illegal acts committed by FBI personnel under his direction. He might have been had he lived longer, or if so many of his potential detractors had not been compromised in his files.

Questions to Consider

- Unlike during Hoover's years, FBI employees are now covered by civil service, and the term of the Director of the FBI is limited to ten years. Do you think those changes have made the FBI more accountable? Why or why not?
- Had J. Edgar Hoover not maintained his secret files would he have been held more accountable?
- The FBI keeps many, perhaps millions, of personal files that are not associated with any criminal investigation. Is this a good idea? Why and why not?
- The President and/or the Attorney General can dismiss (fire) the Director of the FBI without cause at any time. Is such power a good thing? Is it effective in assuring accountability? In what ways?
- Over the years FBI personnel found to have committed illegal acts have been quietly dismissed with no criminal charges being filed. Should laws be passed that would require prosecution of such cases?
- From J. Edgar Hoover's time up to the present day no FBI agent or officer has ever been brought to trial for a criminal act 'sanctioned' by FBI, Justice Department or other federal government persons. Do you think FBI personnel should be

held to the same legal accountability as ordinary citizens? Why or why not?

Chapter 16:
Additional Reading – J. Edgar Hoover/ Federal Bureau of Investigation

Gentry, Curt. *J. Edgar Hoover: The Man and the Secrets.* W.W. Norton & Company, 1992.

Grann, David. *Killers of the Flower Moon: The Osage Murders and the Birth of the FBI.* Doubleday, 2017.

Hoover, J. Edgar. *Persons In Hiding.* Little, Brown, 1938.

Letersky, Paul with Dillow, Gordon. *The Director: My Years Assisting J. Edgar Hoover.* Scribner, 2021.

Also, search the internet for topics such as: FBI history, J. Edgar Hoover, etc.

Case 5:

Mark Zuckerberg/Facebook-Meta

Chapter 17:
Executive Summary

Mark Zuckerberg, was born on May 14, 1984. He grew up in Dobbs Ferry NY, in a large house overlooking the Hudson River.

Zuckerberg attended public schools in Dobbs Ferry until his Junior and senior years at Phillips Exeter Academy in New Hampshire. There he studied the classics and became captain of the fencing team.

In 2002 Zuckerberg entered Harvard as a psychology major, taking computer science as an elective. He lived in a dormitory and joined Alpha Epsilon Pi fraternity. He also met Priscilla Chan; they would marry in 2012.

Early in his freshman year, Zuckerberg built a website where people could see, among other things, who were taking the same courses they were. *Facemash*, the most famous precursor of *Facebook*, was created a year later; Zuckerberg hacked into and took photos from Harvard's data sources. The administration was not amused, but applied only a mild disciplinary action.

Thefacebook officially was chartered on February 11, 2004. In the next few months Zuckerberg and four friends extended the site to more than 100 campuses.

In June Zuckerberg and some of his team left Harvard to spend the summer in 'Silicon Valley.' Zuckerberg was not especially concerned about personal finances; he "believed that success comes from the freedom to fail." He would not return to Harvard.

That summer was manic. Thefacebook expansion to additional campuses continued apace. In July, Zuckerberg restructured Thefacebook in a way that guaranteed him the majority.

Also in July, Sean Parker, a veteran of the social networking scene, was made the President of The Facebook. By the end of the summer Parker had arranged significant financing.

In September Thefacebook introduced two new features – 'Wall' and 'Groups'. Apple, Inc. sponsored a group for its fans, and it agreed to pay $1.00/month for every member, with a minimum of $50,000/month.

Membership, which had reached 200,000 in the summer, shot up to 500,000 in October and exceeded a million users in December. By February 2005, the site was functional at 370 colleges with 2 million active users.

Facebook's membership numbers had flattened by 2005, so Zuckerberg determined to expand Facebook to the general public. A new product was News Feed, which would post on member's pages stories determined by Facebook to be of interest to that particular member.

A high-school version of Facebook, launched in late 2005, was merged with the college version in February 2006. By April, a million high-school students had joined. Open Registration and News Feed went on line in mid-2006.

In 2006, Facebook began allowing outside interests to develop applications using Facebook's platform. Developers' programs would run on Facebook's website, living on pages that were called canvasses. Users would learn about them through the News Feed.

When Facebook users signed up for Outsiders' apps they, in effect, brought their Facebook data with them *and* data on all their 'friends', usually without the knowledge of the 'friends'.

When "Platform" launched in May, Facebook's user base of 20 million was already growing by 100,000 users a day. It would reach 70 million within a year. By the end of the year, Mark Zuckerberg had become one of the youngest billionaires ever.

In 2007, Facebook began developing a "social advertising," whereby what advertisers pay for is less based on clicks for their ads, and more for directing those ads to specific groups or persons. The program had several elements, some of which were rolled out within the year.

'Pages' broke Facebook out of the 'individuals only' mode. Businesses and other entities could henceforth have their own Facebook pages.

'Beacon' allowed selected companies to put invisible monitors on their web pages so that when a Facebook user ordered a product, that purchase was automatically announced to that user's Facebook friends … without consent or even knowledge of the purchaser!

 User pushback soon caused some big advertisers to back out. Two months later Facebook changed to an opt-in option for Beacon, and Zuckerberg publicly apologized. Some two years later a class-action lawsuit caused Facebook to discontinue Beacon altogether (but not the capability).

'Like' button was activated in 2008 to enable people to register, with one click, their acceptance/approval of posts, products, organizations, ideas, etc. Action to 'like' became part of the user's Facebook database and the database of the liked entity. When Facebook expanded the Like button to other sites of the Internet, it became an enormous source of data for Facebook.

'Facebook Connect' was activated in 2008. It allows developers to use Facebook for logging in on their own services and apps, even though the applications might exist outside of Facebook. Users could now use a single login for multiple services. And, as when Facebook users signed up on Outsiders' apps, using one's Facebook login carried one's Facebook data with it.

Platform and Facebook Connect were soon supported by a new Application Programming Interface (API) that Zuckerberg called Open

Graph, which would map the interests and activities of people you know. The first version was announced in 2010.

Facebook used Open Graph to add value to its media platform for advertisers, but the API was also fraught with privacy issues. A Facebook platform operations manager brought that concern to senior executives in 2012. His concerns were dismissed.

In March 2008, Zuckerberg hired Sheryl Sandberg as the new Chief Operating Officer COO) of Facebook. Organizational responsibilities were divided between the two of them; Engineering and programming reported to Zuckerberg, and everything else reported to Sandberg. That organizational framework continued until 2019.

Sandberg and Zuckerberg soon came to understand that capturing information about what people were doing and thinking on the Internet gave Facebook valuable information about people's intent, something advertisers would pay even more for. Facebook had its business model.

In 2009, a formal definition of Facebook values was developed: Focus on Impact, Be Bold, Move Fast and Break Things, Be Open, and Build Social Value. Of those values, one – Move Fast and Break Things – stood out as uniquely Facebook. Zuckerberg was, in a sense, already synonymous with the company.

In 2008 Twitter's growth and influence were exploding. Users on Twitter could freely "cross-post" their tweets to Facebook. Zuckerberg wanted to acquire Twitter, but Twitter's Board rejected his offers. So Facebook incorporated Twitter-like features into News Feed; it replaced the Wall with a Twitterized News Feed.

These and related changes transformed News Feed into a viral engine of vast significance for advertisers and others seeking to influence public opinion.

Quite apart from any competitive aspects, many of the changes affecting privacy were repudiations of long-standing user agreements. These changes seemed to give Facebook freedom to do what it wanted with all the personal details that people shared with it, even if their account was closed.

The reaction was almost entirely negative and loud... The Electronic Privacy Information Center, in concert with eight other organizations, made a formal complaint to the Federal Trade Commission. The case was settled in November of 2011. The FTC cited seven specific issues wherein Facebook was charged with violating its user privacy agreements. Facebook agreed to a 20-year period of oversight by outside auditors.

Facebook went public on May 18, 2012. The S-1 prospectus spelled out a stock structure that would keep Zuckerberg in control. Enthusiastic investors set a value for Facebook of $104 billion, the highest value any technology company had yet achieved.

The IPO provided resources for acquisitions; Facebook paid $1 billion in 2012 for photo-sharing competitor Instagram, and $19-22 billion in 2014 for WhatsApp, a mobile-messaging service. Facebook also acquired Oculus, a virtual-reality startup, for $2.7 billion in 2014.

By fall of 2012, the number of active Facebook users had grown to one billion but the price of Facebook stock had dropped. Aggrieved stockholders filed suits which, over the next few years, Facebook, bankers, and NASDAQ would pay millions to settle.

In 2014, Facebook shut down most developers' access to friend-of-friend data, but not for developers that agreed to share their data with Facebook or provide revenue to Facebook. Such developers were given a new version of Open Graph that granted "full friend access." Developers not granted full-friend access were given until April 2015 before access to the friends API was blocked for them.

However, before Facebook closed its doors to outside developers, an academic at Cambridge University plugged into the Open Graph and created a personality quiz in which nearly 300,000 Facebook users participated. Data was harvested from those individuals as well as from their Facebook friends, multiplying the data set to nearly 90 million Facebook users. The academic then turned the data over to Cambridge Analytica (in violation of Facebook's rules for developers).

The data would be used secretly by Cambridge Analytica and its client, the Trump Presidential Campaign, in the 2016 U.S. presidential election.

Several Russian entities set up internet and Facebook identities to interfere with the election. Facebook informed and cooperated with government agencies about the Russian interference, and it informed the two campaigns. But it did not block or take down the fake accounts.

Zuckerberg felt that Facebook should be a forum for uncensored free speech, and with only few exceptions (bullying, for instance) that was what it was in 2016. But many 'liberal' employees grew angry that Facebook was not helping their cause. The story leaked, and was widely shared; the leaker was fired.

Clamor over the Trump campaign's effective use of Facebook to help win the election began before Trump took office, and would grow throughout 2017. Clamor also grew from those who felt that Facebook was biased against Republicans.

The Facebook security team prepared a white paper detailing Russian activity during the election. Their superiors at Facebook directed them to excise all mentions of Russia, which they did. In April 2017 the paper was released to the press.

On March 18, 2018, the *New York Times* and *The Guardian* published front-page exposés of the Cambridge Analytica uses of Facebook user data. On March 20, the Federal Trade Commission announced its investigation of Facebook's compliance with its 2011 privacy consent decree. It deemed the release of user information to Cambridge Analytica to be a violation of the agreement. (A year later, the FTC would fine Facebook $5 billion for the violations.)

On April 10 the United States senate began ten hours of hearings on "Facebook, Social Media Privacy, and the Use and Abuse of Data." The sole witness was Mark Zuckerberg. He delivered Facebook's standard defense that it gave users control over how their data was used and that the company didn't barter data for profit.

At a management meeting in July, Zuckerberg explained that because Facebook had come under investigation and attack from many fronts he would become a "wartime CEO" and assume more direct control over all aspects of the business.

Before the year ended, Zuckerberg characterized election interference as an arms race against foreign and domestic bad actors. Thousands of new employees were hired to help with security and content moderation. They wrestled with fact-checking statements of political persons, especially President Trump. Zuckerberg stood firm by his belief that freedom of speech meant that while Facebook might "flag" some posts as questionable, it must allow posts it might not like, including lies and misinformation.

Friction between Zuckerberg and the founders of Instagram and WhatsApp had been building before 2018. When Facebook acquired these companies Zuckerberg had promised their founders that they would operate independently from Facebook. But as their popularity and metrics grew to significantly challenge the Facebook platform, their independence was eroded, the support they received was curtailed, and even their inclusion in upper management councils was shut off.

Not surprisingly, the founders of WhatsApp and Instagram left in 2018. Zuckerberg admitted he had broken his word, but felt changing business and market conditions made it necessary.

As 2018 came to a close, 2 billion people were using Facebook platforms each day, up 9 percent from 2017. Revenues were up 37 percent, and net income was up 39 percent.

Zuckerberg began 2019 with Facebook people, at last, heading up all Facebook operations. But critics and regulators were increasingly asking why Zuckerberg had been permitted to acquire those properties in the first place.

Early in the year Zuckerberg announced his intention to encrypt and link its three messaging services – Facebook Messenger. WhatsApp and Instagram Messaging. Instagram's 'Stories' feature was soon introduced on all Facebook platforms. Extending Stories to the other platforms was a violation of agreements Zuckerberg had made with its creators when Facebook acquired Instagram.

In 2019 encrypting was a pivot to privacy that alarmed many Facebook people, because it would weaken the ability to monitor messaging on Facebook platforms. But Zuckerberg persisted. In a blog:

> he revealed that Facebook would focus on creating safe spaces for private conversations. In the past, users were largely encouraged to post on their own pages and those of their friends. The content then appeared in their News Feed … a kind of virtual town hall. Now Zuckerberg wanted people to move to the privacy and security of the equivalent of their living rooms. It was a continuation of Facebook policies that had increasingly encouraged people to join groups.
>
> Zuckerberg explained in the post that the company would also encrypt and link its three messaging services … The "pivot to privacy" … triggered alarm among Facebook's security experts and some executives, who felt... Zuckerberg was effectively weakening Facebook's ability to serve as a watchdog ...

Two months later the now-private Facebook groups were spreading a doctored video of House Speaker Nancy Pelosi in which her speech had been slowed down to make her appear drunk. Other social media took the video down, and Facebook was able to take a majority of the posts down. But not all. The encryption and privacy shift made that almost impossible. Zuckerberg made the final call to leave it up. His position is "When something is misinformation, meaning it's false, we don't take it down … Because we think free expression demands that the only way to fight bad information is with good information."

In January 2020, Facebook began to create a center for information about COVID-19 from the Centers for Disease Control and Prevention, and the World Health Organization. Fact-checking tools would be used to correct conspiracy theories.

The COVID-19 efforts and accompanying public relations boosted Facebook's public image, but that image was again put to the test beginning in April when President Trump held a briefing in which he suggested that disinfectants and ultraviolet light might be treatments for Covid-19. Though the comments were discounted by medical professionals, they went viral on Facebook and Instagram.

In May, Facebook activated The Facebook Oversight Board – an independent final-appeal body regarding decisions on content.

On May 29, Trump posted a message on his Facebook and Twitter accounts about the 'George Floyd' protests bringing violence to many American cities. Included in one of his posts was the comment "Any difficulty and we will assume control but, when the looting starts, the shooting starts." Twitter put a warning label on Trump's post, which brought pressure on Facebook to do likewise.

After much discussion within Facebook and a call from Trump, Zuckerberg agreed to not remove the post or take action against Trump's account. Facebook employees were incensed at Zuckerberg's position. Emails and postings openly criticized him.

Zuckerberg dealt almost exclusively with related questions during his weekly Q&A meetings that month, and he didn't change his position. Part of the problem was that the most extreme behavior was taking place in closed or private groups, which Facebook had promoted for years.

Facebook's AI algorithms were enhanced to the point that they detected and blocked up to 90 percent of posts containing objectionable language. But the 10 percent that weren't caught by algorithms amounted to millions of posts each day to be detected by manual human methods, an impossible task.

In August, a police shooting of a Black man in Kenosha, Wisconsin led to days of violence and two deaths. Violence that continued for several days and spread to other cities across America was incited, largely, by posts on Facebook.

One day after the November 3rd election Zuckerberg approved an emergency temporary change to the News Feed algorithms such that people would see more posts originating from sources deemed trustworthy, and fewer from sources that promoted false news or election conspiracy stories.

> For five days after the vote, Facebook felt like a calmer, less divisive place. "We started calling it 'the nicer News Feed,'" said one member of the election team. "It was this brief glimpse of what Facebook could be..."
>
> But by the end of the month, the old algorithm was slowly transitioned back into place ... quietly, executives worried how conservatives would respond if a number of prominent right-wing outlets were permanently demoted. There was also concern that ... users were spending less time on the platform ... The team was told that Zuckerberg would approve a moderate form of the changes, but only after confirming that the new version did not lead to reduced user engagements.
>
> "The bottom line was that we couldn't hurt our bottom line," observed a Facebook data scientist who worked on the changes. "Mark still wanted people using Facebook as much as possible, as often as possible."

Though ballot counting in many jurisdictions engendered much controversy, Trump lost the election. The Senate met on the afternoon of January 6, 2021, to confirm the election results.

> Before noon, thousands of people gathered at the Ellipse, near the White House, to hear Trump speak... He concluded his address with a call to his supporters: "We're going to walk down Pennsylvania Avenue ... and we're going to the Capitol and we're going to try and give ... our Republicans, the weak ones ... the kind of pride and boldness that they need to take back our country. As the speech ends, crowds start to drift towards the Congress building, about a mile and a half away, where they are met by police barriers...
>
> More than six hours after the storming of the building, senators returned and resumed the day's business of certifying the results of the 2020 presidential election.

Tens of thousands of Facebook user-posted and re-posted pictures and messages that supported and cheered the rioters.

Zuckerberg came under pressure from many directions to permanently ban Trump from Facebook. But instead of making a final determination, on January 21 he handed the decision over to The Facebook Oversight Board; he could now avoid accountability for that decision and many to come.

On August 19, 2021, the Federal Trade Commission (FTC) filed an amended antitrust complaint against Facebook.

On October 21, 2021, Facebook's name was changed to Meta Platforms, Inc.

Chapter 18:
We Know Best

Facebook changed its name to Meta Platforms, Inc. in 2021. For the year ending 12-31-21 its total revenues were $117.9 billion, 98 percent from advertising on its four social-media platforms: Facebook, Instagram, Messenger and WhatsApp. Net income was $46.8 billion. From its inception in 2004 to the present time, the company has been virtually synonymous with its principal founder, controlling stockholder and CEO, Mark Zuckerberg.

Mark Elliot Zuckerberg, second child of Edward and Karen Zuckerberg, was born on May 14, 1984. He grew up with his parents and three sisters in Dobbs Ferry NY, a Westchester County suburb of New York City, in a large house overlooking the Hudson River. The family lived on the second floor, above Dr. Zuckerberg's dental offices.

Zuckerberg's father was an early adopter of computer technology, adapting an Atari 800 to keep patient records in the early 1980s. That computer had been replaced with an IBM PC by the time Mark was born, but his father kept the Atari and let Mark play with it as a tyke.[a] When Zuckerberg was ten, his father bought him a first edition of *C++ For Dummies*, a computer language for creating web applications.

At age 12 Zuckerberg wrote a software program for messaging among the computers at home (every member of the family had one) and at his father's dental practice. He called it "Zucknet" and signed it "Mark Zuckerberg Production", a tagline he would later use on early

---

[a] *Facebook; The Inside Story*, Chapter 1, Steven Levy.

versions of his social media platform. About the same time, while in the sixth grade, Zuckerberg got his own IBM clone, a Quantex 486DX.

Zuckerberg attended public elementary schools in Dobbs Ferry. Then, after two years at nearby Ardsley High School, he transferred to Phillips Exeter Academy in New Hampshire for his junior and senior years. There he studied the classics and was active in sports; he became captain of the fencing team.

He continued to write programming including, with fellow student Adam D'Angelo as a collaborator in a senior project, the *"Synapse Media Player."* Among other things, *Synapse* allowed users to download and share music. Zuckerberg and D'Angelo were reportedly offered millions for this package, which they turned down; *Synapse Media Player* remained freely available.

Facebook was, arguably, born at Exeter, but the 'father' was not Mark Zuckerberg.

> Its creator was a senior named Chris Tillery ...
>
> Tillery's real legacy as an Exonian came from exporting a binder of student headshots and captions known as the Photo Address Book to the ... digital realm ...
>
> Thus was the Exeter Facebook sanctioned, and Tillery released it to the school's entire population, which included Mark Zuckerberg ...
>
> Tillery stopped his involvement with Thefacebook program after graduating from Exeter. His next step was Harvard University. So he was present at the school ... when an online facebook suddenly appeared and swept through the school like a tornado. He wasn't surprised to see that it was created by Mark Zuckerberg. Even in his limited contact with Zuckerberg at Exeter, Tillery noticed that the intense young man had "big, big ambition."[a]

In 2002 Zuckerberg entered Harvard as a psychology major, taking computer science as an elective. He lived in a dormitory, Kirkland

---

[a]   Ibid.

House, and joined Alpha Epsilon Pi fraternity. He also met Priscilla Chan; they would marry in 2012.

Zuckerberg's interest in psychology surely affected his computer programming, which had become his second nature. Early in his freshman year, while most residents of Kirkland House were away at an outing, Zuckerberg downloaded the Harvard course catalog. He used it to build a website where people could see, among other things, who were taking the same courses they were. The website became popular at Harvard.

Facemash, The most famous precursor of *Facebook*, was created a year later.

> In the last week of October 2003, during one mid-term weekend, Zuckerberg … decided to have some fun by creating a prank website. For three straight days he coded and came up with a website which he called Facemash … a page that compared Harvard students not on the basis of their academic achievements, but on the basis of their looks. He sourced the photographs of students from the university's online resources. Two photographs chosen randomly were placed next to each other … The heading above the photos read "Who's hotter? Click to choose."
> … he sent the link for Facemash … to a few friends for their feedback … Within two hours, it had spread like wildfire and was all over the campus.[a]

Zuckerberg had hacked into and taken photos from Harvard's data sources, and the school was flooded with complaints from students who objected to their photos being used without their permission. The computer service department charged him with breaching security and violating individual privacy. Harvard was not amused. Nevertheless, Zuckerberg was not expelled; the administration applied a milder disciplinary action.

---

[a] *Mark Zuckerberg: The Making Of The Greatest*, The Formative Years, Abha Sharma.

Zuckerberg was unfazed by the episode, displaying a stoicism that would distinguish him after more serious misdeeds with astronomically higher stakes.[a]

In late 2003, three Harvard seniors who were working on a website they would call the *Harvard Connection* lost their programmer and contacted Zuckerberg for help.

The three seniors approached Mark Zuckerberg sometime in late November 2003. They met in the dining hall of Kirkland House and discussed their idea with him. Apparently, Zuckerberg showed enthusiastic interest in the idea... They exchanged emails where he appeared to be eager to work on the project and he also communicated that it wouldn't take much time.

In December, there weren't many interactions between Zuckerberg and the Harvard Connection trio, with Zuckerberg remaining mostly unapproachable ... in the period from December 2003 to January 2004, Zuckerberg stopped working on the Harvard Connection. Instead, he started working on his own project ...[b]

The Harvard Connection trio ultimately sued (the name of their website by then had changed to ConnectU.com), and Facebook settled in 2008 for $65 million.

Zuckerberg registered Thefacebook.com on January 11, 2004. ("Facebook.com was not available to him at the time; it had been registered earlier by someone else.) On February 4, Thefacebook was officially opened. Membership and exposure was limited to students enrolled at Harvard.

In the next few months Zuckerberg recruited four friends – Dustin Moskovitz, Chris Hughes, Andrew McCollum and Eduardo Saverin – to join in Thefacebook venture. Saverin put money into the project

---

[a]   *Facebook; The Inside Story*, Chapter 2, Steven Levy.
[b]   *Mark Zuckerberg: The Making Of The Greatest*, Starting Up, Abha Sharma.

and, in return, assumed the title of cofounder.[a] They immediately began expanding Thefacebook to other college campuses. Within a few months the team had expanded Thefacebook to more than 100 campuses.[b]

In June 2004, Zuckerberg and some of his team left Harvard to spend the summer in 'Silicon Valley'; they rented a house in Palo Alto, California. Saverin went to work for Lehman Brothers in New York. Muskovitz and Hughes had summer internships and would come later. Zuckerberg was not especially concerned about personal finances. Even then he "believed that success comes from the freedom to fail."[c] Before they left, Zuckerberg told the student newspaper:

> "My goal is not to have a job. Making cool things is just something I love doing, and not having someone tell me what to do or a timeframe in which to do it is the luxury I am looking for in my life ..."[d]

That summer was manic. Zuckerberg not only added to Thefacebook through his programming, he completed WireHog, a website for file/photo sharing. WireHog didn't last long, but many of its capabilities were later incorporated into Facebook. Thefacebook expansion to additional campuses continued apace, but in a controlled manner; every expansion was preceded by addition of servers and other infrastructure necessary to handle the new subscribers without network slowdown, thus avoiding mistakes made by competitors. Zuckerberg also restructured Thefacebook.

---

[a] *An Ugly Truth; Inside Facebook's Battle For Domination*, Chapter 2, Sheera Frankel and Cecilia Kang.
[b] *Facebook; The Inside Story*, Chapter 3, Steven Levy.
[c] *Mark Zuckerberg: The Making Of The Greatest*, Starting Up, Abha Sharma.
[d] *Harvard Crimson*, June 10. 2004.

> In July 2004 ... Zuckerberg incorporated a new company, which essentially purchased the LLC he had formed with Saverin. The arrangement allowed Zuckerberg to redistribute shares in a way that guaranteed him the majority, while sinking Saverin's stake from roughly 30 percent to less that 10 percent. Saverin protested the decision and later sued for compensation.[a]

One of the most important events of that summer was Mark Zuckerberg's meeting Sean Parker. Several years older than Zuckerberg, Parker was a veteran of the social networking scene. He had co-founded Napster and founded Plaxo, but was no longer involved with either. In July, Parker was made the President of Thefacebook, and he put his considerable expertise into managing the company's maneuvering in Silicon Valley.

One of Parker's first actions was to reincorporate Thefacebook, Inc. in Delaware on 7-29-2004. Zuckerberg owned 51% of the stock. By the end of the summer Parker had arranged significant financing including $37,500 each from Reid Hoffman (founder of LinkedIn), Mark Pincus (founder of Tribe.net) and, for a 10% ownership stake, $500,000 from Peter Thiel (founder of PayPal).

By the fall Zuckerberg had decided to not return to Harvard.

In September Thefacebook introduced two new features – 'Wall' and 'Groups'. Apple, Inc. sponsored a group for its fans, and it agreed to pay $1.00/month for every member, with a minimum of $50,000/month. This added to the much smaller early advertising revenues to provide Facebook with a steady revenue stream.

Membership, which had reached 200,000 in the summer, shot up to 500,000 in October after college classes began the fall terms, and

---

[a] *An Ugly Truth; Inside Facebook's Battle For Domination,* Chapter 2, Sheera Frankel and Cecilia Kang.

exceeded a million users in December. "By February, 2005, the site was functional at 370 colleges with 2 million active users..."[a]

Investors wanted in. Zuckerberg turned most of them down, especially venture capitalists who would want significant influence in or even control of the company. But he did negotiate seriously with two of them, Don Graham of *The Washington Post* and, later, Jim Breyer of venture capitalist Accel. Graham offered $6 million for 10 percent of Facebook. Breyer offered $12.8 million for 10 percent. After some moral angst (he had informally said 'yes' to Graham), Zuckerberg accepted Breyer's larger offer.

> With the money in the bank ... one of the first orders of business was buying the facebook.com domain ... for $200,000, clearing the way for Thefacebook to become simply Facebook.[b]

By mid-2005 Zuckerberg had refined the vision he had for Facebook.

> In June 2005, (he) gathered his employees and told them what he had in mind for Facebook's second summer.
> A site redesign.
> A photo application.
> A personalized newspaper based on user's social activity.
> An events feature.
> A local business product.
> And a feature that he called I'm Bored, which would give people things to do on Facebook.
> It was a list that would transform his site from a college directory to the world's premier social utility ...
> Now he had a team of engineers and a base of millions of users ... he knew it was critical to introduce new features that would expand its powers and make it more addictive ...

[a] *Mark Zuckerberg: The Making Of The Greatest*, Scaling Up, Abha Sharma.
[b] *Facebook; The Inside Story*, Chapter 5, Steven Levy.

while the company still kept his own ethic of moving fast
and fixing later ... "Mark would always be the final arbiter
of what went in the product and how it worked ..."[a]

Facebook's membership numbers had flattened in 2005.
Zuckerberg determined to expand Facebook beyond colleges to the
general public. Another top priority was News Feed, which would post
on member's pages news stories determined by Facebook to be of
interest to that particular member. Three priorities were established for
such stories: At the top was stories about that user. Next were to be
stories about people that user likely cared about. Finally, News Feed
would include "a stream of information that could well augment or
even supplant traditional means of news and entertainment."[b]

A high-school version of Facebook, launched in late 2005, was
merged with the college version in February 2006. By April, a million
high-school students had joined.[c]

Open Registration and News Feed went on line in mid-2006. .

> In the last months of 2006, and into 2007, Facebook's flat
> numbers began to rise. "Within a week of launching we'd
> gone from probably fewer than ten thousand people joining a
> day to sixty or eighty thousand people joining a day, and
> then it grew quickly from there," recalls Zuckerberg.
>
> Open Reg allowed billions of users to flock to Facebook.
> And the News Feed would keep them there, making the site
> as totally consuming for everybody as it was for college
> kids... It would also breed bullying, hate, and deadly
> misinformation.[d]

In 2006, Facebook began allowing outside interests to develop
applications using Facebook's platform; developers gained access to

---

[a] Ibid.
[b] *Facebook; The Inside Story*, Chapter 6, Steven Levy.
[c] *Mark Zuckerberg: The Making Of The Greatest*, Evolution of the CEO and the Leader, Abha Sharma.
[d] *Facebook; The Inside Story*, Chapter 6, Steven Levy.

Facebook's user database! After a disappointing start, the product was changed such that developers' programs would actually run on Facebook's website "living on pages that were called canvasses. Users would learn about them through the News Feed."[a]

When Facebook users signed up for Outsiders' apps they, in effect, brought their Facebook data with them along with data on all their 'friends', usually without the knowledge of the 'friends'. New users of these apps agreed that their data could be used, but their 'friends' gave no such permission.

> Zuckerberg understood that Facebook had to honor the trust of its users. But he also believed that the social apps that would emerge would be worth the risk of leaked information...
>
> Facebook did take steps to prevent leakage. Generally, it required developers to … pledge to Facebook that they would not sell or release that data to others … Platform would cement Facebook's status as the dominant company in the social networking world … By allowing others to make use of the accounts of millions of its users, Facebook would become the de facto global arbiter of people's online identities.[b]

'Platform' launched on May 24, 2007. In his introductory speech, Zuckerberg used a new term – "Social Graph."

> *Social graph* refers to the nexus of connections people have in the real world. By expediting connections to those people who were on your friend-and-acquaintance radar, Facebook was unlocking a network you already had, keeping you in close touch with people huddled next to you on this virtual constellation, and drawing lines to those who were one, two, three degrees away. [c]

---

[a]   *Facebook; The Inside Story*, Chapter 7, Steven Levy.
[b]   Ibid.
[c]   Ibid.

Facebook's user base of 20 million was already growing by 100,000 users a day. It would reach 70 million within a year.[d] By the end of 2007 Mark Zuckerberg had become one of the youngest billionaires ever.

In 2007, Facebook began developing a concept that Zuckerberg called social advertising, whereby what advertisers pay for is less based on clicks for their ads, and more for directing those ads to specific groups or persons. The program had several elements, some of which were rolled out within the year.

'Pages' broke Facebook out of the 'individuals only' mode. Businesses and other entities could henceforth have their own Facebook pages to promote and support programs, businesses, products, movements, agendas, etc.

'Beacon' allowed selected companies to put invisible monitors on their web pages so that when a Facebook user ordered a product, that purchase was automatically announced to the user's Facebook friends, without the explicit consent or even knowledge of the purchaser. Participating advertisers loved it; Facebook users hated it.

> The only notice that this was happening would be a pop-up warning that gave instructions of the actions needed to disable the feature. If you didn't respond to the warning … Facebook interpreted your nonaction as consent … the entire history of user experience dictated that most users would breeze past that warning.
>
> "There was a big debate whether it should be opt-in or opt-out" … the opt-out side believed that the purchase information should be shared by default because, well, that's what Facebook is all about, sharing by default. If Facebook asked people to express that they wanted the feature, Beacon would never succeed …

---

[d] *Mark Zuckerberg: The Making Of The Greatest,* The Trek to the Top, Abha Sharma.

> "We were fighting about the controls until two a.m. the night before the (announcement)," says Facebook's counsel and privacy chief, Chris Kelly. He was joined by several other executives who warned that bad things could happen if Beacon did not have protections. "Mark basically just overruled everyone," says an executive at the time.[a]

User pushback soon caused some big advertisers to back out. Two months later Facebook changed to an opt-in option for Beacon, and Zuckerberg publicly apologized in a post titled "Thoughts on Beacon."

> They were not happy thoughts ... "I'm not proud of the way we've handled this situation and I know we can do better," he wrote. And here was his final fix: "a privacy control to turn off Beacon completely.
>
> The outcry died down, because few took the opportunity to "proactively opt in," and even fewer were aware that the purchase information was still being passed on to Facebook. Unless you found the privacy control to stop it. The purchases just weren't showing up in people's News Feeds.[b]

Some two years later a class-action lawsuit caused Facebook to discontinue Beacon altogether (but not the capability).

'Like' button was activated in 2008 to enable people to register, with one click, their acceptance/approval of posts, products, organizations, ideas, etc. Action to 'like' became part of at least two databases, the user's Facebook database and the database of the liked entity. When Facebook expanded the Like button to other sites of the Internet, it became an enormous source of data for Facebook.

Just before announcement of these initial social advertising features in October, Facebook and Microsoft struck a deal whereby

---

[a]   *Facebook; The Inside Story*, Chapter 8, Steven Levy.
[b]   Ibid.

Facebook was authorized to freely scrape and exploit data from Microsoft's Hotmail.[a]

'Facebook Connect' was activated in 2008. It allows developers to use Facebook for logging in on their own services and apps, even though the applications might exist outside of Facebook. Users could now use a single login for multiple services. And, as when Facebook users signed up on Outsiders' apps, using one's Facebook login carried one's Facebook data with it.

> Facebook Connect was a step toward making Mark Zuckerberg's company the de facto arbiter of identity on the Internet. Your Facebook persona could be used on thousands of other sites. And since you were logging in with Facebook, Zuckerberg's company would be able to monitor your activity.
>
> Facebook already had thousands of developers, but this would raise the number dramatically. And Facebook would also be sharing information it had about users (who intentionally signed up for apps using Facebook Connect) and friends of users (who had no idea that their information was being passed on to apps that they might never have heard of, let alone signed up for).
>
> What data Facebook gave developers was supposedly dictated by its rules, but ... it turned out that in practice those rules were flexible ... [b]

Platform and Facebook Connect were soon supported by a new Application Programming Interface (API) that Zuckerberg called Open Graph, which would map the interests and activities of people you know. The first version was announced in 2010.

By 2011, Apple and Android had introduced APIs for their mobile phones. Developers flocked to them. Platform was soon obsolete. But not Facebook Connect; used in conjunction with mobile apps running

---

[a]   Ibid.
[b]   *Facebook; The Inside Story*, Chapter 7, Steven Levy.

on Apple or Android, developers gained access to Facebook data that could enable new social features on their apps.

Open Graph helped developers design new features. Facebook would use it to add value to its media platform for advertisers. Open graph was also fraught with privacy issues. Sandy Parakilas, a Facebook platform operations manager, brought that concern to senior executives in 2012, presenting "a PowerPoint that showed how Open Graph left users exposed to data brokers and foreign state actors."[a] Parakilas' concerns were dismissed; he left Facebook soon thereafter.

Facebook filed a relevant patent that same year.

> In 2012, Facebook filed for a U.S. patent for *"Determining user personality characteristics from social networking system communications and characteristics."* Facebook's patent application explained that its interest in psychological profiling was because "inferred personality characteristics ... may be used for targeting, ranking, selecting versions of products, and various other purposes" ... Facebook was interested in using it for increased sales of online advertising."[b]

In March, 2008, Zuckerberg hired Sheryl Sandberg as the new Chief Operating Officer COO) of Facebook. Older than Zuckerberg and equally driven, Sandberg brought critical business experience to Facebook's management.

> (Their agreement) would set Facebook's structure for the next decade and beyond: what parts of the company Sandberg would be responsible for and what parts would be excluded from her reporting chain. Zuckerberg felt that Sandberg should basically take on things he wasn't

[a] *An Ugly Truth; Inside Facebook's Battle For Domination*, Chapter 8, Sheera Frankel and Cecilia Kang.

[b] *Mindf*ck: Cambridge Analytica And The Plot To Break America*, Chapter 6, Christopher Wylie.

interested in – sales, policy, communications, lobbying, legal, and anything else with a low geek content ...

But the split would result in some odd bifurcation. The engineers creating ad products... reported up to Zuckerberg in an entirely different organization from those who sold ads. Sales was Sheryl country. And the people building the News Feed itself would report to Zuckerberg, while those who would be responsible for the policy decisions of what would be appropriate content to appear on people's feeds would be working for Sandberg.

Ultimately ... all the responsibility fell to Zuckerberg. "Everything that reports to me reports to him because I report to him," Sandberg says...

Still, for the next decade ... Facebook essentially had two organizations: Zuckerberg's domain and Sheryl World. And in no way were those equal.[a]

Coming to Facebook, Sandberg believed in carrying advertising that created demand for advertisers' products. But she and Zuckerberg soon came to understand that by capturing information about what people were doing and thinking on the Internet, Facebook would have valuable information about people's intent, something advertisers would pay even more for. Facebook had its business model.

(Sandberg) crafted an entirely new spin on Facebook's handling of data privacy and repositioned Facebook as a leader on the issue, pointing to how it offered users granular controls over who (the public, friends, selected individuals) could see particular content. Facebook didn't "share" data with advertisers, she asserted ... True, Facebook didn't physically hand over or directly sell data to advertisers, but advertisers were targeting users by age, income, employment, education, and other demographics ... the evidence was clear that the company's profits came from data ...[b]

[a] *Facebook; The Inside Story*, Chapter 9, Steven Levy.
[b] *An Ugly Truth; Inside Facebook's Battle For Domination*, Chapter 3, Sheera Frankel and Cecilia Kang.

In 2009, Zuckerberg directed that a formal definition of Facebook values be developed. A committee of top executives came up with four, which they presented to Zuckerberg: Focus on Impact, Be Bold, Move Fast and Break Things, Be Open. Zuckerberg added a fifth to the list – Build Social Value. "Of those values, one stood out as uniquely Facebook, uniquely Zuckerberg. "Move Fast and Break Things was, in a sense, already synonymous with the company."[a]

It was in this atmosphere that a Zuckerberg strategy concerning competitors emerged: "Identify a company that poses a present or future threat. Try to buy it. And if they don't sell, emulate it."[b]

Twitter was one of those companies. In 2008 its growth and influence were exploding. Users on Twitter could freely "cross-post" their tweets to Facebook. Zuckerberg wanted to acquire Twitter. He invited Twitter's new CEO to a meeting at which he seemingly agreed to a price that was double Twitter's market value. Nevertheless, Twitter's Board rejected the offer, and Facebook sped up efforts to incorporate Twitter-like features into News Feed.

Facebook was already de-emphasizing the Wall, and that process accelerated its replacement with a Twitterized News Feed.

> Till that time, the feed of stories in the feed had been determined by signals that indicated their importance to you in regard to your network of friends … privacy dictated that your posts (had been) distributed to a limited universe, under your control. But now, Facebook was encouraging you to use its News Feed as you used Twitter – to keep up with celebrities and experts in various fields. If you engaged with them, their posts would probably find you …
>
> Facebook … expanded its role from an information and entertainment source about your social network to something that aspired to be your source of *all* your information and entertainment … If you were interested in a

---

[a] *Facebook; The Inside Story,* Chapter 11, Steven Levy.
[b] Ibid.

subject or a person, Facebook would be interested in serving you stories about it. Those seeking to circulate stories more widely on Facebook learned the rewards would come when people reacted to their stories – clicking on them, liking them, or even just having their eyeballs linger on them.[a]

These and related changes transformed Facebook's News Feed into a viral engine of vast significance for advertisers and those seeking to influence public opinion. Facebook no longer benefited from Twitter cross-posts, so it cut them off.

Quite apart from any competitive aspects, many of the concomitant changes affecting privacy were repudiations of long-standing user agreements.

> In December 2009, (Zuckerberg) announced a gutsy move: certain user details previously set to "private" were being switched to "public." That same day, when users logged on to Facebook, they were greeted with a pop-up box asking them to retain the "everyone" setting, the most public option ... many users clicked to consent without understanding the implications. Previously hidden personal information ... was now searchable on the Web. Users started receiving friend requests from strangers. The new settings were cumbersome and opaque; switching back to more private modes seemed especially tricky.[b]

These changes "seemed to give the company total freedom to do what it wanted with all the personal details that people shared with it – even if their account was closed."[c]

The reaction was almost entirely negative and loud... "The Electronic Privacy Information Center, in concert with eight other

---

[a]   Ibid.
[b]   *An Ugly Truth; Inside Facebook's Battle For Domination*, Chapter 3, Sheera Frankel and Cecilia Kang.
[c]   *Facebook; The Inside Story*, Chapter 11, Steven Levy.

organizations, made a formal complaint to the Federal Trade Commission."[a] Zuckerberg was not personally cited. Had he been, he might have become liable for future civil and criminal penalties.

The case was settled in November of 2011. The FTC cited seven specific issues:

- In December 2009, without warning to or approval from users, Facebook changed its website such that information users designated as private was made public.
- Facebook represented that third-party apps that users installed would provide access only to information the apps need to operate. But the apps granted access to nearly all of users' personal data.
- Facebook told users they could restrict sharing of data to specific authorized audiences such as "Friends Only." But such information was also shared with third-party apps used by their friends.
- Facebook had a Verified Apps program that supposedly certified the security of participating apps. No such program existed.
- Facebook falsely promised users that it would nor share their personal information with advertisers.
- Facebook falsely claimed that when users deactivated or deleted their accounts, their photos and videos would be inaccessible.
- Facebook falsely claimed that it complied with the Safe Harbor Framework that governs data transfer between the United States and the European Union.

---

[a]   Ibid.

Facebook admitted no wrongdoing or misrepresentation, but it agreed to a 20-year period of oversight by outside auditors.

In addition to these specific charges, Facebook had a "Verified Application" label that supposedly assured its users that apps carrying this label had been vetted for trustworthiness. In fact, developers simply paid Facebook a fee to get such a label applied to their apps.

On February 1, 2012, Zuckerberg announced Facebook's Initial Public Offering (IPO). It would take place May 18 on the NASDAQ stock exchange. The S-1 prospectus included a personal letter from Zuckerberg in which he spelled out the five Facebook values, including "Move Fast and Break Things." And Zuckerberg admitted Facebook's disastrous mobile status: "We do not currently directly generate any meaningful revenue from the use of Facebook mobile products, and our ability to do so successfully is unproven." The S-1 also spelled out a stock structure that would keep Zuckerberg in control.

> The key factor was keeping himself in control, presumably forever, by creating two levels of shareholders, with the top level – the one where he had the overwhelming majority of shares – given dominance in any vote... Holding 56 percent of the voting shares, Zuckerberg himself would have veto power over anything that other shareholders, or the board of directors, might order.[a]

Despite the caveat and multiple problems the day of the IPO, enthusiastic investors set a value for Facebook of $104 billion, the highest value any technology company had achieved.

The IPO provided resources for acquisitions; Facebook paid $1 billion in 2012 for photo-sharing competitor Instagram, and $19-22 billion in 2014 for WhatsApp, a mobile-messaging service. Facebook

---

[a]   *Facebook; The Inside Story,* Chapter 12, Steven Levy.

also acquired Oculus, a virtual-reality startup, for $2.7 billion in 2014. More would follow.

By fall of 2012, the number of active Facebook users had grown to one billion. But investors who had bought stock at the initial offering price of $35-38 per share were unable to sell for more than $18-19 per share. Aggrieved stockholders in many states filed suit. "Over the next few years, Facebook, bankers, and NASDAQ would pay millions of dollars to settle them."[a]

As revealed in the S-1, mobile users weren't helping Facebook's advertising business model, because the narrow space on mobile devices couldn't display separate ads properly. So, later in 2012 Facebook began integrating ads into News Feed, which allowed them to be seen on mobile devices. "Mobile ads in the News Feed were wildly successful, and would push Facebook's annual revenue into the realms of tens of billions."[b]

In 2014, Facebook shut down most developers' access to friend-of-friend data, but not for developers that agreed to share their data with Facebook or provide revenue to Facebook through ads or other means. Such developers were given a new version of Open Graph that granted "full friend access." At the time, Zuckerberg boasted that the new version of Open Graph was closing a privacy hole.[c] Nevertheless, even developers not granted full-friend access were given a one-year grace period until April 2015 before access to the friends API was blocked for them.

> Just before Facebook closed its doors to outside developers, though, an academic at Cambridge University named Aleksandr Kogan plugged into the Open Graph and created a personality quiz called "thisisyourdigitallife." nearly 300,000

---

[a] Ibid.
[b] Ibid.
[c] *Facebook; The Inside Story*, Chapter 9, Steven Levy.

Facebook users participated. Kogan harvested data from those individuals as well as their Facebook friends, multiplying his data set to nearly 90 million Facebook users. He then turned the data over to a third party, Cambridge Analytica, in violation of Facebook's rules for developers.[a]

The data would be used secretly by Cambridge Analytica and its client, the Trump Presidential Campaign, in the 2016 U.S. presidential election.

The election was traumatic for Facebook, its officers and employees. Zuckerberg had carefully avoided any disclosure of his political leanings. However, his example was not followed by Facebook officers and employees, many or most of whom were avid Democrats; "Sandberg ... was rumored to be on a short list for a cabinet position in the likely eventuality of a Clinton administration."[b]

In early March, Facebook's security team noticed that Russians were using Facebook to interfere with the presidential campaign. They informed Facebook's General Counsel, but their reports were not passed up to Zuckerberg and Sandberg. "Over the years, the security team had largely been sidelined by the two leaders, who didn't take an active interest in their work or solicit their reports."[c]

Facebook informed and cooperated with government agencies about the Russian activity, and it informed the two campaigns. But it did not block or take down the fake accounts.

Facebook had ... no policies for what to do if a rogue account spread stolen emails across the platform to influence U.S. news coverage. The evidence was clear: Russian hackers posing as Americans were setting up Facebook

---

[a] *An Ugly Truth; Inside Facebook's Battle For Domination*, Chapter 8, Sheera Frankel and Cecilia Kang.

[b] *An Ugly Truth; Inside Facebook's Battle For Domination*, Chapter 4, Sheera Frankel and Cecilia Kang.

[c] *An Ugly Truth; Inside Facebook's Battle For Domination*, Chapter 5, Sheera Frankel and Cecilia Kang.

groups and coordinating with one another to manipulate U.S. citizens. But Facebook didn't have a rule against it.[a]

Zuckerberg felt that Facebook should be a forum for uncensored free speech, and with only few exceptions (bullying, for instance) that was what it was in 2016. But many employees grew angry that Facebook was not helping their cause.

> Employee anger with Zuckerberg was steadily rising as Trump's presidential ambitions shifted from a fantasy to a credible possibility. On March 3, a Facebook worker … entered a question for the next all-hands meeting. "What responsibility does Facebook have to help prevent a President Trump in 2017?" By mid-morning the next day, his question had received enough votes from employees to make it to the short list of questions for Zuckerberg.
>
> Facebook's corporate communications team panicked. If the question were made public, Facebook would live up to its reputation as a company of liberal Democrats. It would look like the platform was biased against Trump …
>
> They advised him to avoid answering the question. He should focus instead on Facebook's commitment to free speech...
>
> That afternoon, Zuckerberg redirected his answer, again, to his belief in free expression.[b]

But the story leaked anyway, and was widely shared. "In Facebook's eleven years of operations, internal conversations, especially Zuckerberg's all-hands meetings, had been considered sacrosanct."[c] The leaker was soon identified and fired.

Clamor over the Trump campaign's effective use of Facebook to help win the election began before Trump took office, and would grow throughout 2017. Clamor also grew

---

[a]   Ibid.
[b]   Ibid.
[c]   Ibid.

from the right, especially that Facebook was biased against Republicans. Zuckerberg was asked about this by Steven Levy in early 2018.

> "If you have a company that is ninety percent liberal – that's probably the makeup of the Bay area – I do think you have some responsibility to make sure that you go out of your way and build systems to make sure that you're not unintentionally building bias in... "
>
> Part of Zuckerberg's discomfort arises from his preference for less oversight. Even while acknowledging that content on Facebook can be harmful or even deadly, he believes that free speech is liberating. "It is the founding ideal of the company," he says. "If you give people a voice, they will be able to share their experiences, creating more transparency in the world. Giving people the personal liberty to share their experiences will end up being positive over time."
>
> Still, it was clear that Zuckerberg did not want the responsibility of policing the speech of more than 2 billion people. He wanted a way out ... "I do not view myself or our company as the authorities on defining what acceptable speech is."[a]

Zuckerberg resolved to have visited all 50 states by the end of 2017, and he would accomplish that goal. Before getting much into that travel, he wrote a long manifesto on *Building Global Community*. In it he specified the areas to which Facebook should be contributing.

> Bringing us all together as a global community is a project bigger than any one organization or company, but Facebook can help contribute to answering these five important questions:
>
> - How do we help people build **supportive communities**?
> - How do we help people build a **safe community?**

---

[a]   *Facebook; The Inside Story*, Chapter 17, Steven Levy.

- How do we help people build an **informed community**?
- How do we help people build a **civically-engaged community**?
- How do we help people build an **inclusive community**?

> My hope is that more of us will commit our energy to building the long term social infrastructure to bring humanity together. The answers to these questions won't all come from Facebook, but I believe we can play a role. Our job at Facebook is to help people make the greatest positive impact while mitigating areas where technology and social media can contribute to divisiveness and isolation.[a]

Zuckerberg's travels during 2017 often took him away from the office and limited his availability to the press and critics of Facebook's role in the elections. The trips included low-key visits with 'real' Americans and local politicians. They dovetailed with high-profile events such as an address at the Harvard commencement that spring, and Facebook's first "Community Summit" in Chicago where he brought together "350 or so unpaid administrators of Facebook groups … to attend workshops, share tips, and cheer loudly …

> Zuckerberg appeared as an unbilled speaker, and the audience went wild … *The meaningful groups like the ones you people administer*, he said, *were the most valuable things on Facebook...* He wanted everybody on Facebook in one of those groups.
> Then he shared a surprise. Right then and there he was changing Facebook's entire *mission*. It was no longer just connecting the world. From this point forward it was "Give people the power to build community and bring the world closer together." The refinement was almost an admission that Facebook's blind chase for growth had created a formless mass, ripe for manipulation.[b]

---

[a]   https://www.vox.com/2017/2/16/14640460/mark-zuckerberg-facebook-mani-festo-letter

[b]   *Facebook; The Inside Story*, Chapter 15, Steven Levy.

The Facebook security team prepared a white paper detailing the Russian activity during the election. Their superiors at Facebook directed them to excise all mentions of Russia, which they did. In April 2017 the paper was released to the press.

Zuckerberg understood that Facebook had to change. Complaints focused overwhelmingly on News Feed. "The popularity of the service, and Zuckerberg's ambitions to make the feed an indispensable source of personalized information, had put an impossible burden on the stream of stories."

> Though in theory scrolling could go on for thousands of posts, people only viewed a handful at a time, so the race for top ranking was a vicious contest, determined by a scoring system beyond the grasp of a single human being ... Facebook evolved its EdgeRank algorithms to determine which posts had the highest ranking, but eventually the system ... evolved into a complicated digital gumbo of more than 100,000 signals. The weights and balances were the result of a never-ending series of experiments, conducted by data scientists working with the News Feed team ... success was measured in terms of ... building and maintaining the user base.
>
> The drawbacks of such a system were best expressed by former Google interface engineer Tristan Harris ... his argument was that the traditional methods of maintaining attention ... had reached a new dimension of toxic addictiveness with the digital tools and artificial-intelligence breakthroughs of the twenty-first century. He considered News Feed and other "infinite scrolls" the worst offenders, Facebook being the worst of the worst.
>
> ... the News Feed team rejected the idea that their daily labors were steps toward annihilating the human race. But the election and its aftermath forced them to deal with the fact that the News Feed could be ... bad for users.[a]

---

[a] Ibid.

On Yom Kippur 2017 (September 29-30), Zuckerberg posted a personal note of atonement to his millions of followers: "For those I hurt this year, I ask forgiveness and I will try to do better. May we all be better in the year ahead, and may you all be inscribed in the book of life."

More than two billion users would be active on Facebook by the end of 2017.

On March 18, 2018, the *New York Times* and *The Guardian* published front-page exposés of the Cambridge Analytica uses of Facebook user data, including in the 2016 presidential campaign. The coordinated stories were based on information from whistleblower Christopher Wylie; Wylie had been pivotal in the design of CA's use of Facebook data for influencing elections in America, the United Kingdom and other countries.

On March 20, the Federal Trade Commission announced its investigation of Facebook's compliance with its 2011 privacy consent decree. It deemed the release of user information to Cambridge Analytica to be a violation of the agreement. (A year later, the FTC would fine Facebook $5 billion for the violations.)

That same day Facebook's employees were informed that the company had opened its own investigation of Cambridge Analytica. But challenges to that internal investigation included the reality that many employees who had been involved with CA were no longer with Facebook. Moreover, British authorities had seized CA's servers (just ahead of Facebook).

> The first order of business, as Zuckerberg saw it, was to play catch-up. He ordered staff to shut down external communications ... He next directed Sandberg and the legal and security teams to scour emails, memos, and messages among Facebook employees, Kogan, and Cambridge Analytica to figure out how the company had lost track of its own data ...

> Zuckerberg fixated on technical details … The breach stemmed from his side of the business … Still, privately, he fumed at Sandberg. During their regular Friday meeting, he snapped that she should have done more to head off the story … The expectation that Sandberg could, or should, be held responsible for the crisis was unrealistic … "Cambridge Analytica came from a decision in the product organization that Mark owned... the decision rested with Mark," one former employee observed . ..
>
> Five days after the scandal broke, Zuckerberg agreed to let a CNN reporter into (Facebook) for an interview. The CEO began on a familiar note of contrition. "This was a major breach of trust, and I'm really sorry that this happened," he said … The company would begin an audit of all the apps that could have possessed and retained sensitive data, he assured CNN's Laurie Segall.
>
> But when Segall asked why Facebook didn't make sure back in 2015 that Cambridge Analytica had deleted the data, Zuckerberg bristled … "I'm used to when people legally certify they're going to do something, they do it."[a]

On April 10 the United States senate began ten hours of hearings on "Facebook, Social Media Privacy, and the Use and Abuse of Data." The sole witness was Mark Zuckerberg, who was well prepared and answered a wide range of questions.

> For the most part, Zuckerberg stuck to the script... And he delivered Facebook's standard defense that it gave users control over how their data was used and that the company didn't barter data for profit. "We do not sell data to advertisers. What we allow is for advertisers to tell us who they want to reach. And then we do the placement."[b]

And, in a *Washington Post* story, he apologized.

[a] *An Ugly Truth; Inside Facebook's Battle For Domination*, Chapter 8, Sheera Frankel and Cecilia Kang.

[b] *An Ugly Truth; Inside Facebook's Battle For Domination*, Chapter 9, Sheera Frankel and Cecilia Kang.

His apology is as straightforward as it can be: 'It was my mistake, and I'm sorry ... I started Facebook, I run it, and I'm responsible for what happens here.'[a]

At a management ("M Team") meeting in July, Zuckerberg discussed his leadership philosophy. He began by reviewing the history of Facebook since its founding. He observed that "Up until this point, the social network had faced obstacles with competition but had enjoyed a clear runway of growth and goodwill from the public, buoyed by the techno-optimism of the past two decades."[b] During those years he had been a "peacetime leader." However, because Facebook had come under investigation and attack from many fronts – "the poster child for irresponsible, at all costs growth "[c] – he was changing his leadership style. He would no longer focus just on products. He would be a "wartime CEO" and assume more direct control over all aspects of the business."[d]

Before the year ended, Zuckerberg characterized election interference as an arms race against foreign and domestic bad actors; thousands of new employees were hired to help with security and content moderation. They wrestled with fact-checking statements of political persons, especially President Trump. Zuckerberg stood firm by his belief that freedom of speech meant that while Facebook might "flag" some posts as questionable, it must allow posts it might not like, including lies and misinformation.

On November 14, the *New York Times* published a story that outlined how Facebook had deflected and denied the truth about Russian election interference, including hiring an opposition research

---

[a] *Mark Zuckerberg: The Making Of The Greatest*, The Man and the World: The Film, Abha Sharma.

[b] *An Ugly Truth; Inside Facebook's Battle For Domination*, Chapter 10, Sheera Frankel and Cecilia Kang.

[c] Ibid.

[d] Ibid.

firm to pursue its critics. Sandberg took a lot of heat, but Zuckerberg stood by her.

> At a Q&A that month, an employee asked Zuckerberg whether he had considered firing any of the chief executives for their failures. Zuckerberg faltered momentarily, then responded that he had not. He gave Sandberg, who was seated in the audience, a small smile as he added that he still had trust in his leadership team to steer the company through the crisis.[a]

Friction between Zuckerberg and the founders of Instagram and WhatsApp had been building before 2018. When Facebook acquired these companies Zuckerberg had promised their founders that they would operate independently from Facebook, simply benefiting from Facebook's resources. For several years, that's what happened. But as their popularity and metrics grew to significantly challenge Thefacebook platform, their independence was eroded, the support they received was curtailed, and even their inclusion in upper management councils was shut off.

Not surprisingly, WhatsApp co-founder Brian Acton left Facebook in 2017. His co-founder Jan Koum left in 2018. Instagram's founders Mike Krieger and Kevin Systrom left in 2018. Zuckerberg admitted he had broken his word, but felt changing business and market conditions made it necessary.

> When speaking about the success of Instagram he made it a point to note that while the co-founders did a good job, their success was equally due to Facebook's support ... He told me he now advises young entrepreneurs not to give in to pressure and sell their companies if they feel that those companies have potential to succeed independently ... "Does that mean that (Instagram's) Kevin and Mikey made a mistake by selling to you?" I asked him.

---

[a]   Ibid.

He paused for a moment … "On the one hand, I think they would've done a good job; they're very talented and could have built the business to be worth more than a billion dollars … On the other hand, I really do think that without the work that Facebook has done … I don't even think that they'd be half as big as they are today."[a]

In 2019 Facebook would introduce 'Stories' on all of its platforms. Up to then, Stories had been a feature unique to Instagram. Extending Stories to the other platforms was a violation of agreements Zuckerberg had made with the its creators when Facebook acquired Instagram.

As 2018 came to a close, "The reporters kept digging and writing, the regulators kept investigating, the courts kept deposing, and the public was still thinking about whether it should #deletefacebook."[b] But Facebook metrics didn't seem to suffer much. By year end 2.0 billion people were using Facebook platforms each day, up 9 percent from 2017. Revenues were up 37 percent, and net income was up 39 percent. Both Monthly Average Users (MAU) and Daily Average Users (DAU) were up about 2 percent worldwide (for the United States and Canada, both metrics were essentially unchanged or slightly down).[c]

Zuckerberg began 2019 with his people, at last, heading up all Facebook operations; the work of melding those operations would proceed without any heel-dragging by reluctant founders. But critics and regulators were increasingly asking why Zuckerberg had been permitted to acquire those properties in the first place.

Calls for antitrust action and investigations against Facebook came from all directions.

---

[a] *Facebook; The Inside Story*, Chapter 19, Steven Levy.
[b] *Facebook; The Inside Story*, Chapter 18, Steven Levy.
[c] Facebook 2018 10-K Annual Report.

By mid-2019, Congress, state, and federal agencies were actively pursuing antitrust investigations against Facebook ... By October, forty-six states and the District of Columbia had joined the investigations, while the FTC and DOJ were both gearing up their own inquiries. The House of Representatives issued a sweeping subpoena ... Meanwhile, presidential candidates were inveighing against the company.[a]

Hearings were held. And nothing substantive happened; Facebook's lobbying prevailed.

In early 2019 Zuckerberg announced his intention to encrypt and link its three messaging services – Facebook Messenger. WhatsApp and Instagram Messaging.

In a blog post titled "A Privacy-Focused Vision for Social Networking" he revealed that Facebook would focus on creating safe spaces for private conversations. In the past, users were largely encouraged to post on their own pages and those of their friends. The content then appeared in their News Feed ... a kind of virtual town hall. Now Zuckerberg wanted people to move to the privacy and security of the equivalent of their living rooms. It was a continuation of Facebook policies that had increasingly encouraged people to join groups.

Zuckerberg explained in the post that the company would also encrypt and link its three messaging services ... "I believe the future of communication will increasingly shift to private, encrypted services where people can be confident what they say to each other stays secure and their messages and comment won't stick around forever ..." The "pivot to privacy" ... triggered alarm among Facebook's security experts and some executives, who felt... Zuckerberg was effectively weakening Facebook's ability to serve as a watchdog ..."[b]

---

[a] *Facebook; The Inside Story*, Chapter 19, Steven Levy.
[b] *An Ugly Truth; Inside Facebook's Battle For Domination*, Chapter 11, Sheera

Two months later the now-private Facebook groups were spreading a doctored video of House Speaker Nancy Pelosi's meeting with Sheryl Sandberg. In the video Pelosi's speech had been slowed down to make her appear drunk. Other social media took the video down, and Facebook was able to take a majority of the posts down. But not all. The encryption and privacy shift made that almost impossible. Facebook executives engaged in intense discussions about how and whether to completely remove the video. "On Friday, 48 hours after the video first surfaced, Zuckerberg made the final call. He said to leave it up."[a] Weeks later, Sandberg "echoed her boss's now familiar position on speech: 'When something is misinformation, meaning it's false, we don't take it down … Because we think free expression demands that the only way to fight bad information is with good information."[b]

In June Facebook unveiled a plan for its own digital currency similar to BitCoin. It partnered with 27 other companies including Mastercard, Visa and PayPal in an association called "Diem." The cryptocurrency, named "Libra," was ultimately deemed to not be politically viable. It was discontinued in January 2022, and the unique blockchain technology was sold.

COVID-19 and U.S. Presidential politics dominated social media during 2020. In January, Facebook began to create a center for information from the Centers for Disease Control and Prevention, and the World Health Organization. "Fact-checking tools to label misinformation would be used to correct conspiracy theories about

---

Frankel and Cecilia Kang.
[a] Ibid.
[b] Ibid.

COVID-19."[c] Facebook was among the first companies to mandate that employees work from home.

The COVID-19 efforts and accompanying public relations boosted Facebook's public image, but that image was again put to the test beginning on April 23. President Trump held a briefing on that day, in which he suggested that disinfectants and ultraviolet light might be treatments for Covid-19. Though the comments were discounted by medical professionals, they went viral on Facebook and Instagram.

In May, Facebook activated the Facebook Oversight Board by appointing its first 20 members – academicians, civil rights experts, former political leaders. The board would function as an independent final appeal body regarding Facebook's decisions on content.

On May 29, Trump posted a message on his Facebook and Twitter accounts about the 'George Floyd' protests bringing violence to many American cities. "Trump wrote that he was concerned about the protests and was in contact with Minnesota Governor Tim Walz to offer the assistance of the U.S. military. Included in one of his posts was the comment "Any difficulty and we will assume control but, when the looting starts, the shooting starts."[a] Twitter put a warning label on Trump's post, which brought pressure on Facebook to do likewise.

After much discussion within Facebook and a call from Trump, Zuckerberg agreed to not remove the post or take action against Trump's account.

> Zuckerberg justified the position in a post on his Facebook page. He found Trump's comments personally offensive, he wrote, "But I'm responsible for reacting not just in my personal capacity but as the leader of an institution committed to free expression."

---

[c] *An Ugly Truth; Inside Facebook's Battle For Domination*, Chapter 14, Sheera Frankel and Cecilia Kang.

[a] Ibid.

Zuckerberg's post was shared widely within the company, along with a clip from a Fox News interview... in which he seemed to criticize Twitter's approach to Trump. "We have a different policy I think, than Twitter on this," Zuckerberg had said, "I just believe strongly that Facebook shouldn't be the arbiter of the truth of everything that people say online."[a]

Facebook employees were incensed at Zuckerberg's position. Emails and postings openly criticized him.

"The hateful rhetoric advocating violence against Black demonstrators by the U.S. President does not warrant defense under the guise of freedom of expression," Robert Traynham, a senior Black employee and director of policy communications, wrote on the Tribe group for Black@Facebook. "Along with Black employees in the company, and all persons with a moral conscience, I am calling for Mark to immediately take down the President's post advocating violence, murder and imminent threat against Black people."[b]

Zuckerberg dealt almost exclusively with related questions during his weekly Q&A meetings that month, and he didn't change his position. "Part of the problem was that the most extreme behavior was taking place in closed or private groups,"[c] which Facebook had promoted for years.

The protests continued into the summer and spread widely outside of Facebook. Calls for a boycott on Facebook advertising led to major advertisers joining the protests.

Facebook's AI algorithms were enhanced to the point that they detected and blocked up to 90 percent of posts containing objectionable language. But the 10 percent that weren't caught by

---

[a]   Ibid.
[b]   Ibid.
[c]   Ibid.

algorithms amounted to millions of posts each day to be detected by manual human methods, an impossible task.

In August Facebook took down some far-right QAnon posts deemed leading to violence, and it also announced that it would remove groups related to the far-left Antifa. Nevertheless, a police shooting of a Black man on August 23 in Kenosha, Wisconsin led to days of violence and two deaths.

On the night of the shooting rioting crowds set fires to cars and trucks and other property. Police used tear gas and rubber bullets to control and disperse crowds. Mostly peaceful demonstrations were held the next day, August 24, but groups arriving during the day were intent on violence; they were coming because, in part, of hundreds of posts on Facebook urging people, left and right, to come to Kenosha.

> The Kenosha Guard, a citizen militia organization with a Facebook group, created an event page named "Armed Citizens to Protect our Lives and Property" on August 24, and by the next evening the page had over 5,000 users. The Kenosha Guard hosted a gathering for militia members to choose locations in the city to protect. Sheriff Beth stated that the presence of militia members created confusion and complicated the situation. Facebook removed the group and page on August 26.[a]

Violence that continued for several days and spread to other cities across America was incited, largely, by posts on Facebook.

Around a week before the first shooting in Kenosha, Facebook had begun "a policy banning exactly these types of extreme groups and militias. But the Kenosha Guard page hadn't yet been taken down because," Zuckerberg said, of "an operational mistake." The explanation satisfied neither the public nor Facebook employees.

---

[a] https://en.wikipedia.org/wiki/Kenosha_unrest

In October, Facebook announced a comprehensive ban of Qanon, a policy banning Holocaust misinformation, and it was removing thousands of militia groups.

> Zuckerberg was pivoting away from long-held beliefs on free speech, but no one at Facebook ... articulated it as a coherent change in policy. In a Q&A with employees on October 15, he pushed back on the idea that he was shifting his principles: "A bunch of people have asked, well, why are we doing this now? ... does this reflect a shift in our underlying philosophy?... The basic answer is that this does not reflect a shift in our underlying philosophy or strong support of free expression. What it reflects is, in our view, an increased risk of violence and unrest.[a]

November 3rd was election day. One day after the election Zuckerberg approved an emergency temporary change to the News Feed algorithms such that people would see more posts originating from sources deemed trustworthy, and fewer from sources that promoted false news or election conspiracy stories.

> For five days after the vote, Facebook felt like a calmer, less divisive place. "We started calling it 'the nicer News Feed,'" said one member of the election team. "It was this brief glimpse of what Facebook could be." Several people on the news team asked whether the "nice News Feed could be made permanent.
> But by the end of the month, the old algorithm was slowly transitioned back into place ... quietly, executives worried how conservatives would respond if a number of prominent right-wing outlets were permanently demoted. There was also concern that Facebook's changes had led to a decrease in sessions; users were spending less time on the platform ... The team was told that Zuckerberg would approve a moderate form of the changes, but only after

---

[a]   *An Ugly Truth; Inside Facebook's Battle For Domination*, Chapter 14, Sheera Frankel and Cecilia Kang.

confirming that the new version did not lead to reduced user engagements.

"The bottom line was that we couldn't hurt our bottom line," observed a Facebook data scientist who worked on the changes. "Mark still wanted people using Facebook as much as possible, as often as possible."[a]

Though ballot counting in many jurisdictions engendered much controversy, Trump lost the election. The Senate met on the afternoon of January 6, 2021, to confirm the election results.

Before noon, thousands of people gathered at the Ellipse, near the White House, to hear Trump speak at a "Save America" rally. He concluded his address with a call to his supporters: "We're going to walk down Pennsylvania Avenue ... and we're going to the Capitol and we're going to try and give ... our Republicans, the weak ones ... the kind of pride and boldness that they need to take back our country. As the speech ends, crowds start to drift towards the Congress building, about a mile and a half away, where they are met by police barriers...

More than six hours after the storming of the building, senators returned and resumed the day's business of certifying the results of the 2020 presidential election."[b]

The riot, which involved more than 2,000 people, continued for several hours. One protester was killed by Capitol police. On Facebook, tens of thousands of users posted and re-posted pictures and messages on Facebook supporting and cheering the rioters. Facebook executives and personnel in California watched in horror as events unfolded.

As Zuckerberg and his executives debated what to do, a chorus was growing across different Tribe boards – engineers, product managers, and members of the policy

---

[a] Ibid.
[b] https://www.bbc.com/news/world-us-canada-55575260

team all calling for Facebook to ban Trump from the platform, once and for all …

By mid-afternoon Wednesday, as the last of the rioters was being escorted away from the Capitol, Zuckerberg had made up his mind to remove two of Trump's posts and to ban the president from posting for twenty-four hours...

By Thursday, he had decided that Facebook would extend its ban of Trump through the inauguration. He also ordered the security team to take sweeping action against a number of pro-Trump groups on the platform that had helped organize the the January 6 rally …

"We believe that the public has a right to the broadest possible access to political speech," Zuckerberg posted on Facebook … "but the current context is now fundamentally different, involving the use of our platform to incite violent insurrection against a democratically elected government..."

Zuckerberg ended the post with a mixed message: he was extending the ban on Trump's Facebook and Instagram accounts "indefinitely," which he went on to qualify as "at least the next two weeks …"[a]

Zuckerberg was under pressure from many directions to permanently ban Trump from Facebook. But instead of making a final determination, on January 21 he handed the decision over to the Facebook Oversight Board; he could now avoid accountability for that decision and many to come.

In August 2021, the Federal Trade Commission (FTC) filed an amended antitrust complaint against Facebook. A more detailed version of a previous complaint dismissed in June for insufficient evidence, the new filing alleges that Facebook violated antitrust laws with its acquisition of Instagram and WhatsApp.

On October 21, 2021, Facebook's name changed to Meta Platforms, Inc.

---

[a] *An Ugly Truth; Inside Facebook's Battle For Domination*, Chapter 14, Sheera Frankel and Cecilia Kang.

Figure 18-1. Sign at Meta Platforms headquarters in Menlo Park, California.

Epilogue

Sheryl Sandberg announced in 2022 that she is stepping down as Chief Operating Officer of Meta Platforms effective in the fall. She will continue on the board as a director of the company.

Meta operating results for the quarter ending September 30, 2022, were down sharply from the prior quarter. On November 9, Meta announced its first-ever layoffs in Mark Zuckerberg's letter to employees.

> Today I'm sharing some of the most difficult changes we've made in Meta's history. I've decided to reduce the size of our team by about 13% and let more than 11,000 of our talented employees go. We are also taking a number of additional steps to become a leaner and more efficient company by

cutting discretionary spending and extending our hiring freeze through Q1.

I want to take accountability for these decisions and for how we got here. I know this is tough for everyone, and I'm especially sorry to those impacted.

At the start of Covid, the world rapidly moved online and the surge of e-commerce led to outsized revenue growth. Many people predicted this would be a permanent acceleration that would continue even after the pandemic ended. I did too, so I made the decision to significantly increase our investments. Unfortunately, this did not play out the way I expected. Not only has online commerce returned to prior trends, but the macroeconomic downturn, increased competition, and ads signal loss have caused our revenue to be much lower than I'd expected. I got this wrong, and I take responsibility for that.

In this new environment, we need to become more capital efficient. We've shifted more of our resources onto a smaller number of high priority growth areas — like our AI discovery engine, our ads and business platforms, and our long-term vision for the metaverse. We've cut costs across our business, including scaling back budgets, reducing perks, and shrinking our real estate footprint. We're restructuring teams to increase our efficiency. But these measures alone won't bring our expenses in line with our revenue growth, so I've also made the hard decision to let people go …

Chapter 19:
Analysis and Discussion – Mark Zuckerberg/Facebook-Meta

Facebook/Meta is virtually synonymous with Mark Zuckerberg. Or perhaps the opposite is more the case. Either way, Zuckerberg should be accountable for everything that his company did and does and will do.

Facebook consistently lied to its users and the public as regards privacy of user information. The settlement of the 2011 FTC case illustrated seven specific examples. Facebook was fined and agreed to cease such activities, but they continued. After several years, Facebook was fined $5 billion for violations of the 2011 agreement.

On April 10, 2018, in his opening remarks at a joint hearing before the Senate subcommittees of Commerce and Justice, Zuckerberg read:

> We didn't take a broad enough view of our responsibility, and that was a big mistake. It was my mistake, and I'm sorry. I started Facebook, I run it, and I'm responsible for what happens here.

But, arguably, for much of those hearings and most of the company's existence, he avoided or hedged acceptance of accountability. His almost knee-jerk response to instances of Facebook/Meta's violations of trust has been to apologize with some variation of "I'm sorry this happened. We'll try to do better." Only rarely has he unequivocally accepted responsibility, as he did at the Senate hearings. And in all the materials researched for this case, in only one instance did he say "I am accountable."

This is not to assert that Mark Zuckerberg is duplicitous, in his mind. It is to assert that he is not accountable. How could he be? There is no one to hold him accountable. He arranged through classification of the company's stock that he would be in total control of the company. Four of the six critical accountability conditions are absent as regards Zuckerberg's relationships with Facebook/Meta, its users and the public.

2. There has never been a personal superior-subordinate relationship; Mark Zuckerberg reports to no one.

3. Again, there is not a one-to-one superior-subordinate relationship. While Zuckerberg nominally reports to a group – the Board of Directors, it has no authority over him.

5. Zuckerberg has selected all members of the Board of directors, many of whom are employees. He wields substantial influence over most of those in the group to which he is nominally accountable.

6. The Board of Directors cannot censure, restrain or otherwise significantly affect Zuckerberg. Like employees, Board members who disapprove of any Zuckerberg action must either go along or get out.

Conclusions

Mark Zuckerberg is in total control of Meta Platforms, Inc., just as if he were the sole owner. Moreover, though he is almost certainly an honorable and principled man, his immense wealth makes him virtually immune to the daily reality of most people and, in many respects, even above the law.

There are at least two ways whereby Meta Platforms can be more accountable. One is external, through law and regulation. The other would be internal, through Zuckerberg-initiated company provisions.

Externally, Facebook is subject to existing antitrust laws, and both the Department of Justice[a] and the Federal Trade Commission[b] have announced expanded views of what may constitute "unfair practices."

An FTC process is ongoing, the end result of which could be to break Meta Platforms into several competing companies, as was done with Standard oil in 1911, and AT&T in the 1980s. Or, Congress might impose a regulatory regimen on the internet industry, as it did on the telecom industry prior to AT&T's breakup. Zuckerberg is on record as potentially favoring some regulation.

> I actually am not sure we shouldn't be regulated. You know, I think in general technology is an increasingly important trend in the world, and I think the question is more what is the right regulation, rather than yes or no, should it be regulated.[c]

Mark Zuckerberg's critics call upon him to judge what is hate, or untruthful, or misleading, or just unacceptable content, and to not permit such material on Meta platforms. But Zuckerberg is a staunch believer in freedom of expression and, his detractors point out, has permitted countless posts on Facebook that, instead of bringing people closer together, have divided its users into Balkanized groups of similar-thinking people – tribes – and, worse, have reinforced narrow and hateful thinking.

Many argue that Facebook should construct algorithms and empower panels of experts to judge potential content and make sure

---

[a] https://www.justice.gov/opa/speech/assistant-attorney-general-jonathan-kanter-delivers-remarks-new-york-city-bar-association
[b] https://www.ftc.gov/legal-library/browse/policy-statement-regarding-scope-un-fair-methods-competition-under-section-5-federal-trade-commission
[c] *CNN Money,* March 21, 2018.

nothing 'inappropriate' gets disseminated. Meta/Facebook has done both of those things, spending billions of dollars to satisfy such critics. But to little avail.

Zuckerberg believes the best antidote to 'bad' material is 'good' material. But the problem is how to counter 'bad' material when existing AI algorithms ensure that countering material will not be seen by all those who eventually see the 'bad' posts.

Here's a thought.

Zuckerberg could redirect his engineers to develop algorithms that support a countering model, which would let him reduce spending money on panels of speech judges. Here are a couple of ways the spirit of "equal time" could work and, perhaps, forestall congressional action.

- Allow anyone to buy advertising targeted to exactly the same audience of any specified ad. In other words, if someone sees an advertisement they consider objectionable, they can purchase an ad carrying a "correcting" message and have Facebook post it to the exact same demographic as the objectionable ad.
- To 'debate' a specific individual post, the response ('comment') of anyone seeing the post, not just Facebook users, could be posted to everywhere the original post appeared, both originally and as forwarded.

In other words, use Meta's engineering strengths to develop a feature/product that enables Zuckerberg's philosophy while increasing user involvement and ad revenue. (Reportedly, such an approach has been discussed within Meta. However, no actions have been taken because of studies indicating that when a strongly-held view is attacked or even just challenged, holders of such views increase commitment to the view; it becomes more firmly entrenched.)

Questions to Consider

- Should Meta Platforms, Inc. be required to divest one or more of its platforms such as Instagram, WhatsApp or Messenger? If not, why not? If so, why and which?
- Suppose Mark Zuckerberg did not have absolute veto power over any decision of the Board of Directors. Would that have improved accountability?
- Suppose Facebook/Meta was not protected by Section 230 from civil liability for what was allowed or disallowed on its platforms. Might that have improved accountability? Why or why not?

Chapter 20:
Additional Reading – Mark Zuckerberg/Facebook-Meta

Beahm, George (editor). *Mark Zuckerberg: In His Own Words*. B2 Books, 2012, 2018.

Frenkel, Sheera and Kang, Cecilia. *An Ugly Truth: Inside Facebook's Battle for Domination*. HarperCollins, 2021.

Levy, Steven. *Facebook: The Inside Story*. Blue Rider Press, 2020.

Sharma, Abha. *Mark Zuckerberg: The Making Of The Greatest*. Rupa Publications, 2019.

Wylie, Christopher. *Mindf*ck: Cambridge Analytica And The Plot To Break America*. Random House, 2019.

Also, search the internet for topics such as: Facebook, Mark Zuckerberg, Meta … etc.

Conclusions

and

Current Applications

Chapter 21:
Conclusions

The heads of many or most very large organizations are virtually unaccountable for their actions. If they report to boards of directors, they're inclined to dilute or diminish the board's authority over them. In the case of government entities, some establishing laws explicitly define them as 'independent' and essentially non-accountable, and for others, Justice declines to prosecute many wrongdoings.

Certainly, many or most organization heads strive to maintain personal accountability. Nevertheless, some wield power over their superiors through financial, virtual blackmail and other extra-legal means. Plausible deniability is commonly arranged when illegal or unethical methods are employed to achieve ends.

Financial resources enable the very wealthy to evade significant accountability for their direct or indirect actions; the magnitude of their wealth gives pause to those who might otherwise bring actions against them.

How can we tell if an organization is too big? In plainest terms, *an organization is too big if its chief executive is not truly accountable for all its actions,* regardless of the reasons. Effective accountability requires that *all* six conditions be present.

1. The responsibilities of the subordinate must be unambiguous.
2. The superior-subordinate relationship must be personal.
3. The superior-subordinate relationship must be one-to-one.
4. The superior-subordinate relationship must include timely direct communication between superior and subordinate.

5. The subordinate must not wield control or undue influence over people to whom he or she is accountable.
6. The superior must have real authority to censure, restrain or otherwise affect the subordinate's well-being up to and including employment termination or legal action.

Government entities and social media are given special protections in the United States against civil actions, especially through sovereign immunity and section 230.

Sovereign immunity is the legal doctrine holding that the government cannot be sued by individuals without its consent. In the United States, sovereign immunity typically applies to both federal and state governments, including their agencies. Governments may waive sovereign immunity for specified circumstances, and some have. But most have not.

Special attention must be given to the realities of social media. Christopher Wylie, founder and then whistle-blower of Cambridge Analytica, encapsulates.

> ... over centuries the law has developed several fundamental presumptions about human nature. The most important of these is the notion of human agency as an irrefutable presumption in the law – that humans have the capacity to make rational and independent choices on their own accord. It follows that the world does not make decisions for humans, but that humans make decisions inside of that world.
>
> The notion of human agency serves as the philosophical basis for criminal culpability, and we punish transgressors of the law on the grounds that they made a condemnable choice ... human laws regulate human acts, and not the motivations or behaviors of their surroundings ...
>
> We can already see how algorithms competing to maximize our attention have the capacity to not only transform cultures but redefine the experience of existence.

Algorithmically reinforced "engagement" lies at the heart of our outrage politics, call-out culture, selfie-induced vanity, tech addiction, and eroding mental well-being. Targeted users are soaked in content to keep them clicking ...

The underlying ideology within social media is not to enhance choice or agency, but to narrow, filter, and *reduce* choice to benefit creators and advertisers. Social media herds the citizenry into surveilled spaces where the architects can track and classify them and use this understanding to influence their behavior ...

Facebook may say: If you don't like it, don't use it. But there are no comparable alternatives to the dominant players on the internet, just as there are no alternatives to electric, telecommunications, or water companies. To reject the use of platforms like Google, Facebook, LinkedIn and Amazon would be to remove oneself from modern society.

These companies ... have done everything in their power to become a necessary part of most people's lives. Getting users to click "accept" after presenting them with a novella's worth of dense legalese (almost twelve thousand words in Facebook's case) is nothing but *consent washing...* No one opts out of these platforms, because users have no other choice but to accept.[a]

Social media are protected from legal accountability in the United States. Section 230 of the U.S. Code protects "Good Samaritan" blocking and screening of offensive material. "No provider ... of an interactive computer service shall be treated as the publisher or speaker of any information provided by another information content provider." Nor shall they be liable on account of "any action voluntarily taken in good faith to restrict access to or availability of material that the provider ... considers to be obscene, lewd, lascivious, filthy, excessively violent, harassing, *or otherwise objectionable* (italics added), whether or not such material is constitutionally

---

[a] *Mindf*ck; Cambridge Analytica And The Plot To Break America*, chapter 12, Christopher Wylie.

protected …" In practice, these provisions have been interpreted that social media services can block access to any post with impunity. They are not accountable. They can't be sued.

Accountability for the person heading an organization often evaporates; it's the very nature of a chief executive's position that most accountability conditions applicable to employees are not present. It is testimony to the integrity of the men and women in these top positions that most maintain personal accountability in spite of the corrupting nature of the power they have. It is also true that some abuse their power no matter what precautions may be taken, and especially if they're protected from accountability by law or circumstance.

So we should consider instituting changes that may minimize such abuses. In the end, *the chief executive should be held accountable for all actions of his or her organization.*

Chapter 22:
What To Do About It

Complete accountability of all chief executives can't be ensured. However, **each private and public organization can strengthen accountability of its Chief by adopting rules that prohibit the chief executive or any employee from sitting on any board or body to which he or she reports.** Organizations could also adopt private versions of some of the following suggested provisions for legal adoption.

Congress and the states can enact changes to federal and state laws intended to motivate many chief executives to behave in a more accountable fashion. Six legislative actions should be considered:

Imputed Culpability: Make it a matter of law that the chief executive of any organization is responsible for acts of subordinates or agents on behalf of the organization, and is punishable in the same degree as the actual perpetrator. Under such a law, chief executives would no longer be shielded by lack of paper trail or plausible deniability, etc. Such provision would also get to those offending executives for whom usual punishments amount to "pocket change."

Benefit limitations: Make it a matter of law that no manager or supervisor in any organization, including the chief executive, may be granted bonuses or increased compensation during or following a year in which anyone within their sphere of responsibility is convicted of a felony on behalf of the organization. If such compensation has been paid before said conviction, recipient(s) of such compensation shall be required to repay it to the organization.

Modify Immunity Provisions: FBI, CIA and other government agents get away with breaking laws because District Attorneys, etc., don't prosecute, often citing sovereign immunity or prosecutorial discretion. Enable citizens to require prosecutions in such cases.

Modify Section 230: Remove the words "or otherwise objectionable" from the wording in Section 230(c)(2).

Revive "Equal Time": Enact a social-media equivalent of the "equal time" rule once required of broadcasters, such that any political candidate can request equal coverage for a rebuttal to any post by or on behalf of his/her opponent, and if any user finds a post to be substantially untrue or just misleading, the user can request equal coverage for a rebuttal post. Require the social media, upon receiving such a request, to allow the complainant to submit a rebuttal or comparable 'correcting' post *that will immediately appear in the news feed of every user who received the offending post.*

Enhance Antitrust Laws: The Clayton Antitrust Act outlaws "mergers and acquisitions when they may substantially reduce competition," and social media concerns are included within this provision. But the Sherman Antitrust Act is ambiguous to the realities of social media.

From the Sherman Act the first sentence of the related U.S. Code provides that "Every person who shall monopolize, or attempt to monopolize, or combine or conspire with any other person or persons to monopolize any part of the trade or commerce among the several States ... shall be deemed guilty of a felony ..."

Social media should be explicitly included, perhaps by inserting "or electronic communications" between "commerce" and "among" in the first sentence of the Code.

Enacting any or all of these suggestions won't affect organizations whose leaders are already assuring their own accountability. And they won't eliminate all abuses. But they will improve the accountability of the chief executives at many of America's private, public and government organizations.

Chapter 23:
Additional Reading – Conclusions and Current Applications

Hawley, Josh. *The Tyranny of Big Tech*. Regnerny Publishing, 2021.

Horton, Thomas R. *The CEO Paradox: The Privilege and Accountability of Leadership*. AMACOM, 1992.

Hyde, Safritz. *Introducing Public Administration, 9Th Edition*. Routledge, 2016.

Wilson, James Q. *Bureaucracy: What Government Agencies Do And Why They Do It*. Basic Books, 1991

Wu, Tim. *The Curse of Bigness: Antitrust in the New Gilded Age*. Columbia Global Reports, 2018.

Also, search the internet for topics such as: Sherman Antitrust Act, Clayton Antitrust Act, equal time rule, Accountability of Chief Executives, Unions, etc. In particular, visit websites such as:

https://pitt.libguides.com/usgovinfo/independentagencies
https://en.wikipedia.0rg/
wiki/Independent_agencies_of_the_United_States_government
https://www.dol.gov/general/workcenter/unions-101

Printed in the USA
CPSIA information can be obtained
at www.ICGtesting.com
BVHW042347310723
668015BV00001B/2